PSYCHOLOGY RESEARCH PROGRESS

ANXIETY DISORDERS

RISK FACTORS, GENETIC DETERMINANTS AND COGNITIVE-BEHAVIORAL TREATMENT

PSYCHOLOGY RESEARCH PROGRESS

Additional books in this series can be found on Nova's website under the Series tab.

Additional e-books in this series can be found on Nova's website under the e-book tab.

PSYCHOLOGY RESEARCH PROGRESS

ANXIETY DISORDERS

RISK FACTORS, GENETIC DETERMINANTS AND COGNITIVE-BEHAVIORAL TREATMENT

SHILOH ANGELUS ROMAN
EDITOR

NOVINKA

New York

For permission to use material from this book please contact us:
Telephone 631-231-7269; Fax 631-231-8175
Web Site: http://www.novapublishers.com

Library of Congress Cataloging-in-Publication Data

ISBN: 978-1-63117-392-9

Library of Congress Control Number: 2014932385

Published by Nova Science Publishers, Inc. † New York

CONTENTS

PREFACE

Anxiety is a basic human emotion that everyone experiences at times. Many people feel anxious, or nervous, when faced with a problem at work, before taking a test, or making an important decision. Anxiety is not typically pathological, but commonly adaptive when it facilitates avoidance of danger. Anxiety disorders, however, are different. They can cause such distress that it interferes with a person's ability to lead a normal life. For people with anxiety disorders, worry and fear are constant and overwhelming. This book examines anxiety in children and the tools and methods used to assess anxiety among young children and adolescents. It also explores the role of genetics in anxiety disorders and the connection between anxiety and temporomandibular disorder.

Chapter 1 – Anxiety disorders have been studied quite extensively in children, from presentation to treatment. Cognitive Behavioral Therapy (CBT) has been the most empirically studied treatment for these children and is now considered probably efficacious by the standards set forth by Chambless and Hollon (1998). However, the majority of child anxiety research has been with children age 8 and above. Yet, there is evidence that problematic anxiety is present in younger populations. Further, evidence has demonstrated that interfering anxiety symptoms begin in early childhood and progressively worsened in severity, indicating the need for early intervention for anxious children. The purpose of the current chapter is to review the small but growing empirical literature examining the presentation and treatment of anxiety in this younger population.

Chapter 2 – This chapter provides an overview of current knowledge on the assessment of anxiety disorders in children and adolescents in relation to CBT treatment. Although the dimensional and categorical approaches have often been presented as opposed, today they appear to be compatible, particularly after the publication of version 5 of the Diagnostic and Statistical Manual of Mental Disorders (DSM-5), which overcomes this opposition and uses the two in combination. Nevertheless, a good working knowledge of these theoretical constructs is needed to choose among the many available clinical tools, questionnaires, tests, etc. The abundance and variety of these instruments means that they need to be selected on a case-by-case basis. especially with children, with whom clinical methodology often requires the participation of an external informant (parent, other close adult). Finally, despite the traditional division between the practices used in assessment and therapy, it is now possible, and even essential, to reconcile evaluative and therapeutic approaches on a single dynamic and longitudinal continuum. Here, the authors examine this particular issue in the case of cognitive and behavioral therapies, wherein the role of the various instruments that they survey include the assessment of both of the treated psychopathologies and of the effectiveness of the therapies themselves. The authors offer recommendations for the selection and use of clinical tools in screening and treatment for anxiety disorders in children and adolescents.

Chapter 3 – There is considerable evidence that genetic determinants could play a role in the pathogenesis of anxiety disorders. Linkage studies, association studies and genome-wide association studies (GWASs) have identified genetic profiles associated with anxiety disorders such as panic disorder (PD), post-traumatic stress disorder (PTSD), obsessive compulsive disorder (OCD), generalized anxiety disorder (GAD) and social anxiety disorder (SAD). There is not one specific gene that causes anxiety, but combinations of genes seem to be at play. Furthermore, environmental factors, like stressful life events, may trigger an anxiety disorder more easily in people who have a genetic predisposition to the illness. However, the mechanisms are far from a complete understanding. To date, the most studied genetic variant is the serotonin transporter polymorphism (5-HTTLPR), which has been indicated as a risk factor for anxiety disorders, also affecting relative treatments. Other studies regarding the genetic susceptibility to anxiety disorders have focused on studying variants in neurotrophic genes (e.g., BDNF) and in the hypothalamic-pituitary-adrenal axis (HPA) related genes (e.g., FKBP5, CRHR1, NR3C1). In particular, candidate gene approach studies have investigated variants in genes related to HPA and corticotropin-releasing hormone (CRH) pathways because of their central role in the adaptation of the organism to stress. Finally, investigations of susceptibility genes for anxiety disorders can be helped from the study of the genetic factors underlying personality traits, such as neuroticism and harm avoidance, that constitute risk factors for anxiety disorders. The identification of genetic variants involved in anxiety may have implications for the optimization of therapeutic interventions because they have been largely shown to represent predictors of poorer response.

Chapter 4 – The current decade (2010-2020), which has been dedicated to bone and joint diseases by the World Health Organization, is the right time to pay attention to musculoskeletal diseases of the orofacial system. Musculoskeletal diseases play a very important role at both the individual and the societal level, because they are generally extremely common in today's world. The development of a number of musculoskeletal diseases is closely related to decreasing age and increasing longevity, and is more common in females. Temporomandibular disorders (TMD) are arthrogenic and myogenic disorders in the area of temporomandibular joints (TMJs) and/or masticatory muscles. TMDs show a greater frequency in females, and our open longitudinal study undertaken between 2001 to 2012 confirmed these epidemiological data, i.e., that TMDs are up to four times more frequent. Their main clinical characteristic is musculoskeletal pain and they are one of the most common causes of pain in the stomatognathous system. Magnetic resonance imaging was used as a 'gold standard' tool for diagnosing intra-articular TMD. The prevalence of clinical symptoms in the adult population ranges from 12% TO 42.7% and the need for treatment, from 3% to 9%. The etiopathogenesis of TMD has not been entirely explained and it is characterized by a multifactorial etiology, with a number of mutually interacting physical and psychosocial factors. Moreover, TMD constitutes the most common cause of nondental, musculoskeletal pain in the orofacial region. The biopsychosocial conceptualization of the pain experience is found in the close connection between pain and psychosocial factors. The relationship between the patients' psychological condition and their reaction to experiencing pain is very important, as are the pathophysiological mechanisms of chronic pain whose intensity is often independent of clinical findings. Untreated acute pain can evolve into a chronic form and become a separate illness. Psychosocial factors, as in other musculoskeletal disorders, play a dominant role and therefore the clinical and radiological findings tend to be disproportionate to the symptoms. Anxiety is the most common affective disorder and a great problem for psychiatry and general medicine. A certain degree of anxiety is normal and can serve as a warning signal of an external or internal threat and has lifesaving qualities. The negative effects of anxiety on the improvement of TMD pain complaints have not been completely explained. A psychological assessment was undertaken using Spielberger's State-Trait Anxiety Inventory (STAI) according to age and sex-related reference values. Reversible, non-invasive therapeutic means are the recommended treatment, and dentists most often use the Michigan or stabilization splint. Other frequent options for the treatment of temporomandibular pain require a multidisciplinary approach, which may involve physical therapy and kinesiotherapy, acupuncture, non-steroidal anti-inflammatory drugs, biofeedback and psychotherapy. Anxiety plays a significant role as comorbidity with TMD-related orofacial pain. Regarding the important role of psychological factors in the development of temporomandibular pain, a system of multidisciplinary diagnosis is needed in TMJ diagnostics, such as STAI, a very easy-to-use psychological tool.

In: Anxiety Disorders
Editor: Shiloh Angelus Roman
ISBN: 978-1-63117-392-9

Chapter 1

ANXIETY IN YOUNG CHILDREN: PRESENTATION AND TREATMENT

Amy Przeworski* and Kimberly Dunbeck
Case Western Reserve University, Cleveland, OH, US

ABSTRACT

Anxiety disorders have been studied quite extensively in children, from presentation to treatment (see Albano and Kendall, 2002; Gosch, Flannery-Schroeder, Mauro, and Compton, 2006). Cognitive Behavioral Therapy (CBT) has been the most empirically studied treatment for these children and is now considered probably efficacious by the standards set forth by Chambless and Hollon (1998) (Ollendick, King, and Chorpita, 2006). However, the majority of child anxiety research has been with children age 8 and above. Yet, there is evidence that problematic anxiety is present in younger populations (Côté et al., 2009; Spence, Rapee, McDonald, and Ingram, 2001). Further, evidence has demonstrated that interfering anxiety symptoms begin in early childhood and progressively worsened in severity, indicating the need for early intervention for anxious children (Hirshfeld-Becker and Biederman, 2002). The purpose of the current chapter is to review the small but growing empirical literature examining the presentation and treatment of anxiety in this younger population.

---

* Corresponding author: Amy Przeworski, Ph.D. Department of Psychological Sciences, Case Western Reserve University, 10900 Euclid Avenue, Cleveland, OH 44106. E-mail: axp335 @case.edu. 216-368-5021.

INTRODUCTION

Anxiety disorders, including Social Anxiety, Separation Anxiety, Generalized Anxiety Disorder (GAD), Specific Phobia and Obsessive Compulsive Disorder (OCD), have been studied quite extensively in children, from presentation to treatment (Albano and Kendall, 2002; Gosch et al., 2006). However, the majority of child anxiety research has been done with children age 8 and above despite evidence that children under 8 experience clinically significant anxiety that can greatly impact their lives and developmental trajectory.

Clinically impairing anxiety have been identified in young children at rates similar to that of older children (Egger and Angold, 2006; Lavigne, LeBailly, Hopkins, Gouze, and Binns, 2009). It is estimated that 6 to 9% of children under 6 years old experience a diagnosable anxiety disorder (Egger and Angold, 2006). Anxiety in early childhood may disrupt typical child development and therefore have long-standing implications for children. Thus it is important for anxiety disorder in young children to be identified and treated as soon as possible.

PHENOMENOLOGY OF ANXIETY SYMPTOMS IN YOUNG CHILDREN

Anxiety symptoms appear to load onto disorders in much the same way in preschool children as with older children. Spence et al. (2001) found that preschool anxiety can be identified via confirmatory factor analysis in the form of social phobia, separation anxiety, OCD, fears of physical injury and generalized anxiety.

Such differentiation was also supported by Mian, Godoy, Briggs-Gowan, and Carter (2012) in 2 to 3 year olds. However, one study (Sterba, Egger, and Angold, 2007) supported the diagnostic differentiation of social phobia and separation anxiety disorder in preschoolers but found that depression and generalized anxiety disorders loaded on a single factor.

Anxiety disorders in young children also appear to be stable unless treated. Bufferd, Dougherty, Carlson, Rose, and Klein (2012) found stability of child anxiety disorders from ages 3 to 6 years of age, including specific phobia, separation anxiety, social anxiety, agoraphobia, and selective mutism.

The most common anxiety disorders in young children appear to be specific phobia (0-11.5% of preschoolers, separation anxiety disorder (0.5-5.4%), GAD (0.5-6.5%), and social anxiety disorder (2.0-4.6%), followed by agoraphobia (3.5%), selective mutism (.6-1.5%), and panic disorder (.2%) (Bufferd et al., 2012; Earls, 1982; Egger and Angold, 2006; Gadow, Sprafkin, and Nolan, 2001; Keenan, Shaw, Walsh, Delliquadri, and Giovannelli, 1997; Lavigne et al., 2009). Given the frequency of these anxiety symptoms in young children, it is essential to assess for these disorders and identify symptoms as early as possible. However, it is often difficult for parents to distinguish between anxiety symptoms that are a part of normative child development and those that require intervention.

NORMATIVE DEVELOPMENTAL FEARS

Some degree of anxiety and fear is normative in early childhood. During infancy children show developmentally appropriate fears of loud and sudden stimuli, the loss of support, and heights. By the second half of the first year of life, fear of strangers and novel objects develops (Jersild, 1968; Morris and Kratochwill, 1983). Children between the ages of 1 and 4 years old commonly fear separation from their parents (Dashiff, 1995). The fear usually appears during the latter 6 months of the first year of life, peaks at around 18 months of age or after and is fairly common through age 4, when the fear diminishes in most children (Dashiff, 1995). Animals, darkness, and monsters also constitute common fears of toddlers and preschoolers (Campbell, 1986). These fears typically decline dramatically between early and middle childhood, as fears of bodily injury, physical danger, and natural disasters increase (Campbell, 1986). The number of fears reported by children also declines with age (Macfarlane, Allen, and Honzik, 1954).

It is theorized that this change in the content of children's fears and number of fears may coincide with the development of the ability to discriminate between reality and fantasy and with the development of self-concept. Vasey, Crnic, and Carter (1994) found that preschool children can experience worry and report on the cognitive aspects of worry, but the complexity of worry increased with age and cognitive development. Five to six year olds worried about their physical well-being while older children (8-12 years of age) who have a more advanced sense of self-concept, worried about the competence and negative evaluation by others (Vasey et al., 1994).

In contrast to normative fears, fears that become problematic are defined as excessive, persistent, maladaptive fears that are neither age nor developmental stage appropriate and cannot be reasoned away (Murphy, 1985).

Prevalence rates of problematic fears in preschoolers are estimated to be around 3-7% (e.g., Miller, Barrett, and Hampe, 1974). However, in one study of 3 year olds, 12.8% were rated as having severe fears (Richman, Stevenson, and Graham, 1975). It may be difficult to distinguish between normative childhood fears and maladaptive levels of anxiety in young children.

ASSESSMENT

Assessment of anxiety symptoms in young children presents many challenges including limitations in children's ability to identify, describe, and express their emotional states due to their level of cognitive, language and emotional development.

Young children (under the age of 3) are able to identify only primary emotions such as happiness, anger, sadness and fear (Izard, 1994). Preschool age children begin to understand emotions as they relate to themselves (emotions such as shame, pride, and guilt) but cannot describe having two feelings at the same time or blends of emotions (Harris, 1989; Harter, 1977). Preschool children also view experience and expression of emotion as synonymous, meaning they define emotional experiences by outside behavioral manifestations of the emotion rather than recognizing emotions as internal experiences (Nannis, 1985; Nannis and Cowan, 1987).

Young children also struggle to connect past events with current emotions or thoughts (Shirk, 1988) and are likely to attribute events to conscious, concrete reasons or outside forces as opposed to psychological or internal experiences. Additionally, because emotional competence is intertwined with the ability to use emotion descriptive language (Beck, Kumschick, Eid, and Klann-Delius, 2012), it may be difficult for young children to express their emotional experience until they develop the language to express and describe their emotions. These developmental limitations often complicate the identification of anxiety disorder symptoms in children and the render it difficult to make a distinction between normative childhood fears and maladaptive anxiety symptoms in young children.

Self-Report Measures

Few reliable and valid assessment tools exist for assessing anxiety in young children. Children below the age of 8 often have difficulty completing self-report measures without assistance (Beidel and Stanley, 1993). Some have suggested that children may be likely to respond to questions on questionnaires based on their emotional reaction to a statement rather than based on the frequency of the event (King and Gullone, 1990; McCathie and Spence, 1991). However, one study indicated that children as young as 4 years of age can report on their daily emotional states when assessed using a pictorial Likert scale and simplified wording read to them by an assessor (Lagattuta, Sayfan, and Bamford, 2012).

Few attempts have been made to utilize child self-report assessment in young children; however, one measure, the Koala Fear Questionnaire (Muris et al., 2003) has been developed to assess child anxiety via picture representations of Koala bears expressing differing degrees of fear. The Koala Fear Questionnaire yields a total score for fears, has been used in children ages 4-6 years and had good psychometrics (Muris et al., 2003).

Another measure, the Dominic Questionnaire-Revised (Valla, Bergeron, Bidaut-Russell, St-Georges, and Gaudet, 1997), is an interview-based measure in which children hear about a child named Dominic and his emotional and behavioral reactions to life situations and indicate whether they would have felt the same or acted the same if they were in the situation. The measure uses a pictorial scale. The Dominic Questionnaire assesses symptoms of specific phobia, separation anxiety, and generalized anxiety and can be used in children as young as six. The measure has good psychometric properties (Valla et al., 1997).

Parent Report Questionnaires

Most assessments of young children's anxiety symptoms rely on parent report. Many studies of anxiety in young children use general internalizing parent-report measures such as the Child Behavior Checklist (CBCL; Achenbach and Edelbrock, 1983), Infant-Toddler Social and Emotional Assessment (ITSEA; Carter, Briggs-Gowan, Jones, and Little, 2003), and the Strengths and Difficulties Questionnaire (SDQ; Goodman, 1997; Goodman, Meltzer, and Bailey, 1998). While informative, these measures offer limited information on anxiety in particular.

Therefore, some parent-report measures of young child anxiety have been developed. These include: the Revised Preschool Anxiety Scale (Edwards, Rapee, Kennedy, and Spence, 2010), the Fear Survey Schedule Infants-Preschoolers (FSSIP; Warren, Ollendick, and Simmens, 2008) and Children's Mood, Fears, and Worries Questionnaire (Bayer, Sanson, and Hemphill, 2006).

The Revised Preschool Anxiety Scale (Edwards et al., 2010), is a parent-report of 3-5 year olds' social anxiety, separation anxiety, general anxiety, and specific fears. The measure also yields a total scale. Good psychometric properties have been reported (Edwards et al., 2010).

The Fear Survey Schedule Infants-Preschoolers (FSSIP; Warren et al., 2008), is a parent report of fears in children ages 18 months to 5 years. The measure was developed based on the Revised Fear Survey Schedule for Children (FSSC-R; Ollendick, 1983), which is a child self-report for older children (ages 7-18). In the FSSIP, parents rate each fear on a scale of "None," "Some," and "A lot." The measure yields a total fear scale and a high intensity fear score, ''HIFS,'' which indicates the number of fears receiving a rating of "A lot." The FSSIP has good psychometric properties (Warren et al., 2008).

The Children's Mood, Fears, and Worries Questionnaire (Bayer et al., 2006) is a measure of internalizing symptoms, including mood, worry and fears in children ages 2-4 years of age. The measure yields an internalizing scale and a solitary play scale; thus is does not provide information about specific anxiety disorder diagnoses. Preliminary data indicates that the measure has good psychometric properties (Bayer et al., 2006).

Diagnostic Interviews

Diagnostic interviews are also used in some studies examining young children. Most of these interview measures are used in children ages 6 and above; however there are a handful of interviews that may be used for younger children.

Interviews for Children below Age 6

The Berkeley Puppet Interview (Measelle, Ablow, Cowan, and Cowan, 1998) is an interview administered through the use of puppets which assesses psychiatric symptoms in young children. Children's responses are coded on a 7-point Likert-type scale with higher scores representing greater psychopathology. The interview includes scales measuring generalized anxiety and separation anxiety. It has good internal consistency, test-retest reliability, and validity (Ablow et al., 1999).

The Diagnostic Infant and Preschool Assessment (DIPA; Scheeringa and Haslett, 2010) is a diagnostic interview that assesses for the major anxiety, mood, and behavioral disorders in children ages 1-6. Disorder modules are self-contained and clearly separated by diagnosis, rending it easy to identify whether a child suffers from the symptoms of a particular diagnosis. The measure has good initial psychometrics (Scheeringa and Haslett, 2010).

The Kiddie Schedule for Affective Disorders and Schizophrenia for School Age Children-Present and Lifetime Version (K-SADS-P/L; Chambers et al., 1985) is a semi-structured, clinician rated interview that yields DSM-IV diagnoses of mood, anxiety, and behavioral disorders. The interview has good psychometric properties in preschool children (ages 2-5 years) (Birmaher et al., 2009).

The Preschool Age Psychiatric Assessment (PAPA; Egger and Angold, 2006) is a parent-report of preschooler's (ages 2-5 years) psychopathology and includes an assessment of mood, anxiety, and behavioral symptoms. Symptoms are assessed in the 3 months prior to the interview but age of onset (if it occurred prior to the last 3 months) is also assessed. The PAPA has good test-retest reliability (Egger and Angold, 2006); however, questions about the anxiety disorders are not separated by diagnosis and therefore it requires that the assessor apply an algorithm to identify which anxiety diagnosis a child may have.

Interviews for Ages 6 and Above

The Anxiety Disorders Interview Schedule for DSM-IV (ADIS-C-IV; Silverman and Albano, 1996) assesses anxiety, affective, externalizing and substance use disorders in children between the ages of 6 and 17 and has separate parent and child versions. The child and parent versions have been found to be equally reliable for younger children and for child or parent generated diagnoses (Silverman, Saavedra, and Pina, 2001). The measure has good psychometrics and sensitivity to treatment effects (Albano, Marten, Holt, Heimberg, and Barlow, 1995; Kendall, 1994; Silverman et al., 2001; Tracey, Chorpita, Douban, and Barlow, 1997; Wood, Piacentini, Bergman, McCracken, and Barrios, 2002). Although the ADIS-C-IV is designed for older children, the parent report has been used in children ages 3-5 with good interrater agreement (Rapee, Kennedy, Ingram, Edwards, and Sweeney, 2005).

The Child Assessment Schedule (CAS; Hodges, Gordon, and Lennon, 1990; Hodges and Saunders, 1989; Hodges, Saunders, Kashani, Hamlett, and

Thompson, 1990) is a diagnostic interview that was developed to address the difficulty of establishing rapport with children when conducting structured interviews. It uses a conversational format to increase rapport and is low in structure; therefore, it requires highly trained administrators. This interview is used with children between the ages of 6-12 and CAS assesses mood, behavioral, and anxiety disorders. It has good psychometrics (Hodges, Gordon, et al., 1990; Hodges and Saunders, 1989; Hodges, Saunders, et al., 1990; Verhulst, Althaus, and Berden, 1987).

The Children's Yale-Brown Obsessive Compulsive Scale (CY-BOCS; W. K. Goodman, 1991) is a semi-structured interview that assesses OCD severity in children ages 6-17 years. The CY-BOCS consists of one interview that is administered to both the parent and child together or separately. The interview contains separate sections for obsessions and compulsions and yields obsession and compulsion subscale as well as a total score. Scores of greater than 15 on the total score indicate clinically significant OCD. The measure has sound psychometrics (Scahill et al., 1997). The Diagnostic Interview for Children and Adolescents (DICA-R; Herjanic and Reich, 1997) is a semi-structured interview that assesses DSM-IV lifetime diagnoses in children ages 6-17. There are parent, child, and adolescent interviews and a self-administered computerized version. The DICA-R has been used widely in both clinical and epidemiological research (Reich, 2000) and has strong psychometric properties (Boyle et al., 1996; Boyle et al., 1997; De la Osa, Ezpeleta, Doménech, Navarro, and Losilla, 1996; Welner, Reich, Herjanic, Jung, and Amado, 1987). The National Institute of Mental Health Diagnostic Interview Schedule for Children--fourth version (DISC-IV; Fisher et al., 1993; Shaffer, Fisher, Lucas, Dulcan, and Schwab-Stone, 2000) is a structured diagnostic interview for children ages 6-17. Symptoms are assessed for two time periods--the past 4 weeks and 12 months. There is also an optional module that assesses for the presence of lifetime diagnoses. The DISC-IV consists of child and parent versions, each of which takes 70-120 minutes to administer. The DISC-IV was designed to be administered by a lay interviewer, and therefore lacks open ended probes, which would require interpretation by an experienced clinician. Psychometric data on the DISC-IV is sound (Fisher et al., 1997; Shaffer et al., 2000).

Need for Early Intervention

Much as it is necessary for assessment tools to be tailored to the unique developmental needs of young children, it is also necessary for interventions to be tailored to this population in order for early intervention to be efficacious.

Early intervention is important, not only due to the long-term ramifications of suffering from anxiety symptoms and the early age of onset of anxiety disorders in many children, but also due to the emotional and social development that takes place during early childhood. Early childhood is a pivotal stage for children's emotional and social development, during which the building blocks for later interpersonal and regulatory skills are largely developed. Young children develop an understanding of their internal sensations of emotion, the acceptability of emotional expression, and display rules that motivate hiding emotions (Harris, Olthof, and Terwogt, 1981). Through increased separations from their caregivers, young children also learn more independent methods of regulating emotion through behavioral changes and mental manipulations such as attention deployment (Harris et al., 1981). Thus early child development sets the stage for psychological health. Intervening at this early stage may allow children to maximize their resilience, avoid lost developmental opportunities, and prevent a trajectory towards psychopathology. Therefore, Shonkoff and Phillips (2000) emphasize "intervene early, intervene often, and intervene consistently". However, early intervention for anxiety symptoms may require alterations to treatment in order for it to be developmentally sensitive (Choate-Summers et al., 2008; Freeman et al., 2007; Freeman et al., 2008; Kazdin and Weisz, 1998; Ollendick, Grills, and King, 2001).

Interventions for Young Children

Young children may not have the level of abstract thinking necessary to fully benefit from cognitive therapy techniques (Grave and Blissett, 2004). Further, young children are still developing emotional understanding and learning about the acceptability of emotions and are dependent on their relationship with their caregivers to learn emotion-regulation skills. Because of this developmentally appropriate reliance on parents for the socialization of emotion and behavior, young children require a treatment that is uniquely tailored to their developmental level and that targets parent-child interactions which may maintain the child's anxiety symptoms.

The literature examining the efficacy of treatments for young children with anxiety disorders is in its infancy. Most investigations in this young age have focused on Separation Anxiety Disorder, OCD, Social Anxiety Disorder and Selective Mutism and have been from a cognitive-behavioral therapy (CBT) orientation, with attempts to make current CBT treatments for anxiety developmentally appropriate for young children. Some treatment studies have also incorporated play therapy, parent training, and family systems approaches in the treatment of anxiety in young children (Bratton, Ray, Rhine, and Jones, 2005; Choate, Pincus, Eyberg, and Barlow, 2006; Waters, Ford, Wharton, and Cobham, 2009).

MULTIPLE ANXIETY DISORDERS

We are aware of two randomized controlled trials (RCTs) that examined cognitive behavioral treatments for various anxiety disorders in children young children. The first compared parent-only CBT, parent-child CBT and a wait-list control in a sample of children 4 to 8 years old with Specific Phobia, Social Phobia, Generalized Anxiety Disorder, and Separation Anxiety Disorder (Waters et al., 2009). In the parent-child CBT condition children attended 10 group meetings that focused on psycho-education about anxiety, learning relaxation techniques, using positive self-statements, gradually confronting anxiety provoking situations, and learning social skills in developmentally appropriate ways using games and activities. The parent sessions in both the parent-child and parent-only CBT groups were identical and included psychoeducation about anxiety, parenting strategies for managing child anxiety, ways to improve parent-child relationships, strategies for helping children face their fears, training in communication and problem solving as well as promotion of effective coping. Results of the randomized controlled trial indicated that both the parent-only and parent-child CBT groups were more effective than the wait-list control condition when diagnostic criteria and anxiety severity ratings of children and parents were used as the outcome measures. No differences were found between the two treatment groups, though this could have been due to limited statistical power. The study did provide evidence that CBT both with parents only and with children and parents may be effective in treating young children with anxiety.

The second randomized controlled trial examined the treatment of anxious children who were 4-7 years old (Hirshfeld-Becker et al., 2010). This treatment was examined using children with Separation Anxiety Disorder, Social Anxiety Disorder, Generalized Anxiety Disorder, Avoidant Disorder, and Specific Phobia. The treatment called Being Brave: A Program for Coping with Anxiety for Young Children and Their Parents was based on The Coping Cat (Kendall, Kane, and Howard, 1992), a popular manualized treatment for children 8 and older. Being Brave consisted of 14 to 18 sessions. There were 6 parent-only sessions that focused on psychoeducation, anxiety management strategies, parenting skills for parenting an anxious child, and instruction on positive reinforcement of child exposures. These sessions were followed by parent and child sessions in which the therapist helped the child and parent complete exposure exercises to several feared stimuli. Results of this study indicated reduction in anxiety diagnosis and symptom severity and increased coping skills in children receiving the treatment compared to a wait-list control indicating that developmentally appropriate child and parent CBT may be effective in treating young children with various anxiety disorders (Hirshfeld-Becker et al., 2010).

Separation Anxiety

Separation Anxiety Disorder is characterized by inappropriate concern or anxiety regarding separation from a child's attachment figure. CBT consisting of exposure to feared stimuli, relaxation training, modeling, contingent reinforcement of approach behaviors and use of positive self-statements has been shown to be effective for older children with Separation Anxiety Disorder (see Fischer, Himle, and Thyer, 1999).

However, few empirical studies have looked at CBT for separation anxiety disorder in young children in particular. Pincus, Eyberg, and Choate (2005) tailored Parent Child Interaction Therapy (PCIT; Brinkmeyer and Eyberg, 2003) to be applied with young children ages 4-8 with separation anxiety disorder and their parents.

PCIT is a behavioral treatment that was originally designed to treat child behavior problems using parent-child interaction to improve family and child functioning (Eyberg, 1988). PCIT targets parents' overcontrolling behaviors which have been identified as important in anxiety disorders as well as behavior problems (Chorpita and Barlow, 1998; Chorpita, Brown, and Barlow, 1998).

This skills-based approach teaches parents to use differential reinforcement, deliver clear commands to children, and play in positive ways with their children. After establishing positive interactions between the parent and child, the treatment teaches parents to help children approach feared situations and establish firm limits for unacceptable behavior.

PCIT has been adapted for use in young children with separation anxiety disorder (Pincus, Santucci, Ehrenreich, and Eyberg, 2008). This adapted treatment involved directly applying learned skills to anxious situations, for instance, how to praise brave behaviors while ignoring anxious ones. Treatment ranged from 6 to 7 sessions.

Preliminary studies of PCIT for separation anxiety disorder indicate that PCIT is helpful in decreasing separation anxiety symptoms in young children (Choate et al., 2006; Pincus et al., 2005; Pincus et al., 2008). Choate et al. (2006) conducted an open pilot trial with three families with children with separation anxiety disorder (ages 5-8 years) in a multiple baseline study. Results indicated that PCIT reduced child separation anxiety disorder symptoms and disruptive behaviors. A randomized controlled trial is currently being conducted comparing PCIT to a wait list control. Preliminary results indicated that PCIT led to reductions in SAD severity relative to the waiting list (Pincus et al., 2008).

OBSESSIVE COMPULSIVE DISORDER (OCD)

Obsessive-Compulsive Disorder (OCD) has been identified in children as young as three years of age (Hollingsworth, Tanguay, Grossman, and Pabst, 1981; Swedo, Rapoport, Leonard, Lenane, and Cheslow, 1989). Early age of onset and longer duration of OCD symptoms predict higher rates of persistence of OCD at follow-up (Stewart et al., 2004) therefore, early intervention is recommended when symptoms are present in young childhood.

Therapeutic interventions for older children typically consist of psychoeducation, externalizing OCD symptoms, mapping OCD symptoms to identify when the child is in control of symptoms and when OCD is in control, and exposure with response prevention (EX/RP) (Barrett, Healy-Farrell, and March, 2004; de Haan, Hoogduin, Buitelaar, and Keijsers, 1998; M. Franklin, Foa, and March, 2003; M. E. Franklin et al., 1998; March et al., 2004; March and Mulle, 1998; Pediatric OCD, 2004). This therapy package has been demonstrated to be efficacious in numerous randomized controlled trials for children ages 7 and older (e.g., Barrett, Farrell, Dadds, and Boulter, 2005;

Barrett et al., 2004; March et al., 2004; Pediatric OCD, 2004) however, children 8 and younger were underrepresented in those samples relative to older children and adolescents.

To date, we are aware of only one randomized controlled trial of therapy for young children with OCD. Freeman and colleagues (2007, 2008) adapted the exposure and response-prevention-based therapy described above to meet the developmental needs of children ages 5-8. The treatment consists of psychoeducation about OCD in young children, parent education, and exposure with response prevention adapted to fit young children and their parents.

Parent involvement in treatment at home and in session is essential and parents serve the role of coaches during exposure homework exercises. Further, the inclusion of parents in the treatment addresses family accommodation of OCD symptoms that may be occurring. Family accommodation is associated with less parent-child agreement, fewer solution-based strategies, and higher rates of depression in family members (Amir, Freshman, and Foa, 2000) and may be particularly relevant to address in families of young children who, due to the child's level of dependence on parents, are likely to be engaging in accommodation of OCD symptoms.

Freeman and colleagues conducted one randomized controlled trial of the treatment in comparison to a relaxation condition. Results supported the use of CBT for OCD in children ages 5-8 with 50% of those in the CBT condition achieving clinical remission (as compared with only 4 of 20 (20%) children in a relaxation condition (Freeman et al., 2008). A larger randomized controlled trial is currently underway.

Selective Mutism

Selective Mutism (SM) is a psychological disorder in which children do not speak in certain situations despite adequate verbal ability and proper communication in other situations. There is significant evidence that SM is an anxiety disorder and it has been newly classified as one in the Diagnostic and Statistical Manual-4 (DSM-5; American Psychiatric Association, 2013). The age of onset for SM is believed to be before age 5 and treatment usually occurs between ages 6 and 8 (see Pionek Stone, Kratochwill, Sladezcek, and Serlin, 2002) meaning most treatment research on this sample is in younger children. Unfortunately, there has been limited research on effective treatments for children with selective mutism.

Case studies have demonstrated the success from several treatment orientations including cognitive-behavioral, behavioral, psychodynamic, family systems and multimodal (Pionek Stone et al., 2002). Many of these case and small group studies have demonstrated the success of behavioral techniques including contingency management, shaping, stimulus fading, systematic desensitization and self-monitoring (see Cohan, Chavira, and Stein, 2006).

To our knowledge, one randomized controlled trial exists comparing integrated behavior therapy for children with selective mutism and a wait-list control (Bergman, Gonzalez, Piacentini, and Keller, 2013). Participants were 4 to 8 years old and randomly assigned to the treatment or control group. Treatment involved having the child slowly face fears of speaking in various situations, helping parents to positively reinforce speaking behaviors, and teaching children to use positive self-statements when scared to speak. The last few sessions were used to transfer control of exposures to the parent from the therapist to encourage continued progress outside of therapy. Throughout therapy the therapist was in contact with the child's school and attempted to maintain a reward system that involved school behavior as well as behavior at home. Results indicated that Integrated Behavioral Therapy for selective mutism is likely very successful with 75% of children showing an increase in functional speech post-treatment. Exposure based treatment offers a promising avenue for future selective mutism treatment research (Bergman et al., 2013).

SOCIAL ANXIETY DISORDER

The authors are unaware of any treatment studies examining treatment of Social Anxiety Disorder in children under 7 years old (not including the studies mentioned above treating multiple anxiety disorders together). Treatments of older children have shown success using cognitive behavior techniques including: exposure, relaxation, cognitive restructuring, assertiveness training, and social skills training. These skills have been effective in decreasing social anxiety symptoms in both group and individual therapy settings (for a review, see Kashdan and Herbert, 2001). It is possible that such techniques could be made developmentally appropriate for younger children but such treatments have yet to be investigated.

SPECIFIC PHOBIA

To the authors' knowledge no studies have examined the efficacy of treatment for specific phobia in children below age 8. Treatments in older children have found that in vivo exposures to the feared stimulus along with participant modeling of approach behaviors have been found to be the most effective (for a review see Ollendick and King, 1998). Research has also supported the efficacy of one-session exposure, a prolonged session of graduated exposure, for older children (e.g., Ollendick et al., 2009) (e.g., Ollendick et al., 2009). It has been suggested that parental involvement in one-session treatments is no more successful than child only treatments in older children (Öst, Svensson, Hellström, and Lindwall, 2001); however, it is possible that this may not hold for younger children given their greater level of parental dependence. It is possible that in vivo exposure and modeling is effective with younger children but this hypothesis has yet to be investigated.

POSTTRAUMATIC STRESS DISORDER (PTSD)

Most treatment studies of PTSD have focused on school age children; however, a handful of studies have treated young children who suffered trauma. Young children who suffer traumatic events, such as sexual abuse may not develop PTSD or other psychopathology until they have developed a greater understanding of their trauma (McFarlane, Policansky, and Irwin, 1987). When they do develop PTSD, it is unremitting over a 2 year period (Scheeringa, Zeanah, Myers, and Putnam, 2005). Thus, it is common for these symptoms to develop during adolescence or adulthood (Beitchman et al., 1992) and it has been recommended that interventions for young children focus on current symptoms as well as prevention of future symptoms (Berliner and Wheeler, 1987).

In one of the first studies to examine therapy for traumatized young children, Stauffer and Deblinger (1996) examined the effects of an 11 week group CBT for maternal nonoffending caregivers and their young (ages 2-6 years) sexually abused children in an open trial. Treatment consisted of a parents' group that was designed to help parents with their own emotional coping in order to allow them to be more supportive of their children, improve parent-child communication about child's sexual abuse and healthy sexuality, and provide behavioral management skills.

There was an accompanying child group in which the goals were to reduce stigmatization/isolation, increase communication and emotional coping, and provide information about child sexual abuse and the difference between appropriate and inappropriate touching. Results indicated significant decreases in parents' distress and children's sexual behaviors from pre- to post-therapy, with results maintained at a 3-month follow-up. Unfortunately, child PTSD symptoms were not included as an outcome measure in this study.

The research group followed this up with a randomized controlled trial of this treatment versus a supportive therapy in sexually abused children (ages 2-8) and their non-offending maternal caregivers (Deblinger, Stauffer, and Steer, 2001). Both therapies were efficacious, but effects were larger in the CBT group. Mothers in CBT group reported fewer intrusive thoughts regarding their child's sexual abuse and fewer negative emotional reactions to child's sexual abuse. Children in both groups had reductions in PTSD symptoms from pre- to post-therapy.

Similarly, Cohen and Mannarino (1996) conducted a randomized controlled trial of 12 sessions of individual trauma-focused CBT versus play therapy for sexually abused young children (ages 3-6 years old). Trauma-focused CBT consisted of addressing parents' reactions to the abuse, parental ability to provide support to the child, behavior management, management of child anxiety symptoms, assertiveness training for children, and information about appropriate and inappropriate touching. Trauma-focused CBT led to greater reductions in externalizing and internalizing symptoms (Cohen and Mannarino, 1996) which were maintained over one-year follow-up (Cohen and Mannarino, 1997). Similar to Stauffer and Delbinger (1996), no measure of child PTSD was included as an outcome measures in this study, so it is difficult to know whether CBT was efficacious in reducing child PTSD.

Very few published papers have addressed traumas other than sexual abuse in young children. Scheeringa et al. (2007) presented data on CBT with 2 cases of preschool children, one of whom had a motor vehicle accident and another who survived Hurricane Katrina. CBT consisted of relaxation, in session exposure, relapse prevention and caregivers were included in the treatment. The goal of the manuscript was to examine whether children this young could participate in these therapy techniques. Both children were able to participate in the therapy techniques and experienced reductions in PTSD symptoms. Scheeringa, Weems, Cohen, Amaya-Jackson, and Guthrie (2011) conducted a randomized controlled trial of young children (ages 3-7) who had experienced any type of traumatic event and had at least four symptoms of PTSD.

The majority of children in the sample had experienced Hurricane Katrina, chronic and repeated traumatic events, or an acute single blow trauma. Children were randomized to a waiting list or trauma-focused CBT consisting of 12 sessions of psychoeducation, identification of emotions, coping skills, and graded exposure. Mothers were present for 3 of the sessions and observed the other sessions on screens. Results indicated that the intervention group experienced greater reductions in PTSD, but not on depression, separation anxiety, or externalizing symptoms. CBT was also demonstrated to be understandable by children in the sample.

Generalized Anxiety Disorder (GAD)

The authors are unaware of any studies examining the treatment of young children with generalized anxiety disorder (GAD). Few studies have examined the treatment of child GAD in older children (excluding integrated treatments for various anxiety disorders). However, evidence suggests that cognitive restructuring, self-monitoring of worry, self-evaluation, and self-reinforcement are successful techniques for the treatment of GAD in older children. Cognitive behavioral treatments using these techniques have found improvements in child GAD symptoms via self-report, parent report and physiological measures (e.g., Eisen and Silverman, 1999). Effective treatment for young children with GAD may look similar to these treatments but research is needed to confirm this.

Prevention Efforts

A handful of studies have examined prevention efforts in young children at risk for anxiety disorders. LaFreniere and Capuano (1997) randomly assigned anxious/withdrawn preschoolers (ages 31-70 months) to a parent-child intervention or a monitoring alone control condition. The parent-child intervention consisted of 20 sessions, each of which was 90 minutes long) and included psychoeducation, child-directed play, parenting training, and behavior modification. Results indicated no group differences in children's anxious/withdrawn behavior at post-treatment, but parents in the intervention reported reduced levels of intrusive control and children's social competence also improved in this group.

Rapee et al. (2005) examined the effectiveness of a cognitive-behavioral prevention/intervention program for parents of behaviorally inhibited children ages 36 to 62 months. Parents qualified for the study if their children were inhibited, however, over 90% of children met criteria for an anxiety disorder. The program was a 5-session parent education program administered in small groups. Sessions included psychoeducation on anxiety and it's development, explained principles of parent-management and the role of overprotection in the perpetuation of anxiety, explanation of exposure and cognitive restructuring and explanation of vigilance during high-risk times.

Results of this prevention/intervention were inconsistent. There was no significant reduction in anxiety symptoms compared to the wait-list control. However, there was a significant decrease in the number of children who continued to meet diagnostic criteria for a disorder in the treatment group.

Kennedy, Rapee, and Edwards (2009) completed a similar prevention intervention for parents of children high in behavioral inhibition. In this study 8 parent groups were conducted focusing on psychoeducation of anxiety, management of anxiety, parenting skills, reduction of overprotection, introduction of exposure, enhancement of social skills, cognitive restructuring of anxious thoughts, exposure for parents fears, making of coping plans, and relapse prevention. Children whose parents participated in the prevention program showed decreases in the severity of anxiety as well as a decrease in behavior inhibition temperament characteristics.

Dadds and Roth (2008) conducted a universal intervention program for parents of 3 to 7 year olds. This six-session cognitive behavioral prevention focused on empathetic responding, inevitability of stress, positive re-inforcement, behavior management, increasing self-esteem, challenging negative thoughts and problem solving. Results suggested some improvement in anxiety symptoms via teacher report but these results were not confirmed with parent report; rendering it difficult to draw conclusions about the impact of the intervention.

Conclusions and Future Directions

The research on young child anxiety is in its infancy. However, as a field, our understanding of the existence of problematic anxiety in younger children and its demonstrated stability throughout childhood and adulthood has prompted several steps in the right direction.

Several young child assessment strategies now exist to help clinicians determine if fears are developmentally appropriate. Most of these tools are parent-report, with continued exploration into the validity and reliability of self-report and observational tools needed. Existing assessment tools also need more empirical evaluation to ensure their validity in this population.

Many questions remain regarding the treatment of anxiety disorders in young children. Research has indicated that adapting efficacious treatment for older children has been somewhat successful in Selective Mutism, PTSD, and OCD, as has adapting treatments originally designed for disorders other than anxiety disorders, as is the case of PCIT for Separation Anxiety Disorder. Adaptations to make treatment applicable to younger clients include use of pictures, simplified language and integration of play. Some also argue that parents should be more involved with young child treatment as younger children are more dependent on their caregivers (e.g., (Amir et al., 2000).

Some of the most notable gaps in the research are the treatment of GAD, Specific Phobia and Social Anxiety Disorder. While these disorders have been addressed in two studies using an integrated anxiety protocol, the authors are unaware of studies looking at their treatment independently. The rates of these disorders are estimated to be consistent with that of older children (Angold and Egger, 2006); however, it is possible that developmental differences in younger children would influence the manifestation and expression of these disorders as well as the efficacy of intervention.

For example, cognitive development level may influence the degree to which younger children exhibit negative cognitions or worries that are commonly seen in older children with GAD and social anxiety disorder. Additionally, social-emotional development may influence the degree to which younger children focus on negative evaluation by others and therefore the types of social fears and socially-evaluative situations that prompt anxiety in younger children.

These developmental differences may also influence the methods of treatment and efficacy of various intervention techniques for young children. As such, the lack of empirically tested treatments for these disorders is concerning. Future research should focus on treatment in these populations as well as continue examining the efficacy of treatment in the other young child anxiety disorders. Further, research should examine which techniques are successful with young children and what adaptations are necessary to ensure that interventions are developmentally appropriate. While there have been some studies examining the prevention of anxiety disorders in this young population, the results have been mixed. Some of these studies have shown decreases in anxious symptoms, others have shown decreases in anxiety severity, while some have not (e.g., Dadds and Roth, 2008; Kennedy, Rapee and Edwards, 2009). Further investigation into successful prevention techniques as well as translation of findings into treatment options is warranted. Overall, continued efforts are needed on all fronts in regard to the accurate assessment of and efficacious treatment of young child anxiety.

REFERENCES

Ablow, J. C., Measelle, J. R., Kraemer, H. C., Harrington, R., Luby, J., Smider, N., ... Heffelfinger, A. (1999). The MacArthur Three-City Outcome Study: Evaluating multi-informant measures of young children's symptomatology. *Journal of the American Academy of Child and Adolescent Psychiatry,* 38(12), 1580-1590.

Achenbach, T. M. and Edelbrock, C. S. (1983). *Manual for the child behavior checklist and revised child behavior profile.*

Albano, A. M. and Kendall, P. C. (2002). Cognitive behavioural therapy for children and adolescents with anxiety disorders: Clinical research advances. *International Review of Psychiatry,* 14(2), 129-134.

Albano, A. M., Marten, P. A., Holt, C. S., Heimberg, R. G., and Barlow, D. H. (1995). Cognitive-behavioral group treatment for social phobia in adolescents a preliminary study. *The Journal of nervous and mental disease,* 183(10), 649-656.

American Psychiatric Association. (2013). *Diagnostic and Statistical Manual of Mental Disorderrs (DSM 5)*: American Psychiatric Association.

Amir, N., Freshman, M. and Foa, E. B. (2000). Family distress and involvement in relatives of obsessive-compulsive disorder patients. *Journal of Anxiety Disorders,* 14(3), 209-217.

Barrett, P., Farrell, L., Dadds, M., and Boulter, N. (2005). Cognitive-behavioral family treatment of childhood obsessive-compulsive disorder: Long-term follow-up and predictors of outcome. *Journal of the American Academy of Child and Adolescent Psychiatry,* 44(10), 1005-1014.

Barrett, P., Healy-Farrell, L. and March, J. S. (2004). Cognitive-behavioral family treatment of childhood obsessive-compulsive disorder: a controlled trial. *Journal of the American Academy of Child and Adolescent Psychiatry,* 43(1), 46-62.

Bayer, J. K., Sanson, A. V. and Hemphill, S. A. (2006). Children's Moods, Fears, and Worries Development of an Early Childhood Parent

Questionnaire. *Journal of emotional and behavioral disorders,* 14(1), 41-49.

Beck, L., Kumschick, I. R., Eid, M., and Klann-Delius, G. (2012). Relationship between language competence and emotional competence in middle childhood. *Emotion,* 12(3), 503-514. doi: 10.1037/a0026320.

Beidel, D. C. and Stanley, M. A. (1993). Developmental issues in the measurement of anxiety. *Anxiety across the lifespan: A developmental perspective,* 167-203.

Beitchman, J. H., Zucker, K. J., Hood, J. E., DaCosta, G. A., Akman, D., and Cassavia, E. (1992). A review of the long-term effects of child sexual abuse. *Child abuse and neglect,* 16(1), 101-118.

Bergman, R. L., Gonzalez, A., Piacentini, J., and Keller, M. L. (2013). Integrated Behavior Therapy for Selective Mutism: A randomized controlled pilot study. *Behaviour research and therapy,* 51(10), 680-689.

Berliner, L. and Wheeler, J. R. (1987). Treating the effects of sexual abuse on children. *Journal of Interpersonal Violence,* 2(4), 415-434.

Birmaher, B., Ehmann, M., Axelson, D. A., Goldstein, B. I., Monk, K., Kalas, C., ... Bridge, J. (2009). Schedule for affective disorders and schizophrenia for school-age children (K-SADS-PL) for the assessment of preschool children–a preliminary psychometric study. *Journal of psychiatric research,* 43(7), 680-686.

Boyle, M. H., Offord, D. R., Racine, Y., Szatmari, P., Fleming, J. E., and Sanford, M. (1996). Identifying thresholds for classifying childhood psychiatric disorder: Issues and prospects. *Journal of the American Academy of Child and Adolescent Psychiatry,* 35(11), 1440-1448.

Boyle, M. H., Offord, D. R., Racine, Y. A., Szatmari, P., Sanford, M., and Fleming, J. E. (1997). Adequacy of interviews vs checklists for classifying childhood psychiatric disorder based on parent reports. *Archives of General Psychiatry.*

Bratton, S. C., Ray, D., Rhine, T., and Jones, L. (2005). The Efficacy of Play Therapy With Children: A Meta-Analytic Review of Treatment Outcomes. *Professional Psychology: Research and Practice,* 36(4), 376-390. doi: 10.1037/0735-7028.36.4.376.

Brinkmeyer, M. Y. and Eyberg, S. M. (2003). Parent-child interaction therapy for oppositional children.

Bufferd, S. J., Dougherty, L. R., Carlson, G. A., Rose, S., and Klein, D. N. (2012). Psychiatric disorders in preschoolers: continuity from ages 3 to 6. *The American journal of psychiatry,* 169(11), 1157.

Campbell, S. B. (1986). Developmental issues in childhood anxiety. *Anxiety disorders of childhood*, 24-57.

Carter, A. S., Briggs-Gowan, M. J., Jones, S. M., and Little, T. D. (2003). The infant–toddler social and emotional assessment (ITSEA): Factor structure, reliability, and validity. *Journal of abnormal child psychology,* 31(5), 495-514.

Chambers, W. J., Puig-Antich, J., Hirsch, M., Paez, P., Ambrosini, P. J., Tabrizi, M. A., and Davies, M. (1985). The assessment of affective disorders in children and adolescents by semistructured interview: test-retest reliability of the Schedule for Affective Disorders and Schizophrenia for School-Age Children, Present Episode Version. *Archives of General Psychiatry,* 42(7), 696.

Chambless, D. L. and Hollon, S. D. (1998). Defining empirically supported therapies. *Journal of consulting and clinical psychology,* 66(1), 7.

Choate-Summers, M. L., Freeman, J. B., Garcia, A. M., Coyne, L., Przeworski, A., and Leonard, H. L. (2008). Clinical considerations when tailoring cognitive behavioral treatment for young children with obsessive compulsive disorder. *Education and Treatment of Children,* 31(3), 395-416.

Choate, M. L., Pincus, D. B., Eyberg, S. M., and Barlow, D. H. (2006). Parent-child interaction therapy for treatment of separation anxiety disorder in young children: A pilot study. *Cognitive and Behavioral Practice,* 12(1), 126-135.

Chorpita, B. F. and Barlow, D. H. (1998). The development of anxiety: the role of control in the early environment. *Psychological bulletin,* 124(1), 3.

Chorpita, B. F., Brown, T. A. and Barlow, D. H. (1998). Perceived control as a mediator of family environment in etiological models of childhood anxiety. *Behavior Therapy,* 29(3), 457-476.

Cohan, S. L., Chavira, D. A. and Stein, M. B. (2006). Practitioner review: Psychosocial interventions for children with selective mutism: A critical evaluation of the literature from 1990–2005. *Journal of Child Psychology and Psychiatry,* 47(11), 1085-1097.

Cohen, J. A. and Mannarino, A. P. (1996). A treatment outcome study for sexually abused preschool children: Initial findings. *Journal of the American Academy of Child and Adolescent Psychiatry,* 35(1), 42-50.

Cohen, J. A. and Mannarino, A. P. (1997). A treatment study for sexually abused preschool children: Outcome during a one-year follow-up. *Journal of the American Academy of Child and Adolescent Psychiatry,* 36(9), 1228-1235.

Côté, S. M., Boivin, M., Liu, X., Nagin, D. S., Zoccolillo, M., and Tremblay, R. E. (2009). Depression and anxiety symptoms: onset, developmental course and risk factors during early childhood. *Journal of Child Psychology and Psychiatry,* 50(10), 1201-1208.

Dadds, M. R. and Roth, J. H. (2008). Prevention of anxiety disorders: Results of a universal trial with young children. *Journal of Child and Family Studies,* 17(3), 320-335.

Dashiff, C. J. (1995). Understanding separation anxiety disorder. *Journal of Child and Adolescent Psychiatric Nursing,* 8(2), 27-38.

De Haan, E., Hoogduin, K. A., Buitelaar, J. K., and Keijsers, G. P. (1998). Behavior therapy versus clomipramine for the treatment of obsessive-compulsive disorder in children and adolescents. *Journal of the American Academy of Child and Adolescent Psychiatry,* 37(10), 1022-1029.

De la Osa, N., Ezpeleta, L., Doménech, J., Navarro, J., and Losilla, J. (1996). Convergent and discriminant validity of the Structured Diagnostic Interview for Children and Adolescents (DICA-R). *Clínica y Salud,* 7(2), 181-194.

Deblinger, E., Stauffer, L. B. and Steer, R. A. (2001). Comparative efficacies of supportive and cognitive behavioral group therapies for young children who have been sexually abused and their nonoffending mothers. *Child Maltreatment,* 6(4), 332-343.

Earls, F. (1982). Application of DSM-III in an epidemiological study of preschool children. *The American journal of psychiatry.*

Edwards, S. L., Rapee, R. M., Kennedy, S. J., and Spence, S. H. (2010). The assessment of anxiety symptoms in preschool-aged children: the revised Preschool Anxiety Scale. *Journal of Clinical Child and Adolescent Psychology,* 39(3), 400-409.

Egger, H. L. and Angold, A. (2006). Common emotional and behavioral disorders in preschool children: presentation, nosology, and epidemiology. *Journal of Child Psychology and Psychiatry,* 47(3-4), 313-337.

Eisen, A. R. and Silverman, W. K. (1999). Prescriptive treatment for generalized anxiety disorder in children. *Behavior Therapy,* 29(1), 105-121.

Eyberg, S. (1988). Parent-child interaction therapy: Integration of traditional and behavioral concerns. *Child and Family Behavior Therapy,* 10(1), 33-46.

Fischer, D., Himle, J. and Thyer, B. (1999). Separation anxiety disorder. *Handbook of prescriptive treatments for children and adolescents,* 2, 141-154.

Fisher, P., Lucas, C., Shaffer, D., Schwab-Stone, M., Dulcan, M., Graae, F., ... Gerald, J. (1997). *Diagnostic Interview Schedule for Children, Version IV (DISC-IV). Test-retest reliability in a clinical sample.* Paper presented at the 44th annual meeting of the American Academy of Child and Adolescent Psychiatry, Toronto.

Fisher, P., Shaffer, D., Piacentini, J. C., Lapkin, J., Kafantaris, V., Leonard, H., and Herzog, D. B. (1993). Sensitivity of the Diagnostic Interview Schedule for Children, (DISC-2.1) for specific diagnoses of children and adolescents. *Journal of the American Academy of Child and Adolescent Psychiatry,* 32(3), 666-673.

Franklin, M., Foa, E. and March, J. S. (2003). The pediatric obsessive-compulsive disorder treatment study: rationale, design, and methods. *Journal of Child and Adolescent Psychopharmacology,* 13(2, Supplement 1), 39-51.

Franklin, M. E., Kozak, M. J., Cashman, L. A., Coles, M. E., Rheingold, A. A., and Foa, E. B. (1998). Cognitive-behavioral treatment of pediatric obsessive-compulsive disorder: an open clinical trial. *Journal of the American Academy of Child and Adolescent Psychiatry,* 37(4), 412-419.

Freeman, J. B., Choate-Summers, M. L., Moore, P. S., Garcia, A. M., Sapyta, J. J., Leonard, H. L., and Franklin, M. E. (2007). Cognitive behavioral treatment for young children with obsessive-compulsive disorder. *Biological psychiatry,* 61(3), 337-343.

Freeman, J. B., Garcia, A. M., Coyne, L., Ale, C., Przeworski, A., Himle, M., ... Leonard, H. L. (2008). Early childhood OCD: Preliminary findings from a family-based cognitive-behavioral approach. *Journal of the American Academy of Child and Adolescent Psychiatry,* 47(5), 593-602.

Gadow, K. D., Sprafkin, J. and Nolan, E. E. (2001). DSM-IV Symptoms in Community and Clinic Preschool Children. *Journal of the American Academy of Child and Adolescent Psychiatry,* 40(12), 1383-1392.

Goodman, R. (1997). The Strengths and Difficulties Questionnaire: a research note. *Journal of child psychology and psychiatry,* 38(5), 581-586.

Goodman, R., Meltzer, H. and Bailey, V. (1998). The Strengths and Difficulties Questionnaire: a pilot study on the validity of the self-report version. *European child and adolescent psychiatry,* 7(3), 125-130.

Goodman, W. K. (1991). *Children's Yale-Brown Obsessive Compulsive Scale (CY-BOCS).*

Gosch, E. A., Flannery-Schroeder, E., Mauro, C. F., and Compton, S. N. (2006). Principles of cognitive-behavioral therapy for anxiety disorders in children. *Journal of Cognitive Psychotherapy,* 20(3), 247-262.

Grave, J. and Blissett, J. (2004). Is cognitive behavior therapy developmentally appropriate for young children? A critical review of the evidence. *Clinical Psychology Review,* 24(4), 399-420.

Harris, P. L. (1989). *Children and emotion: The development of psychological understanding*: Basil Blackwell.

Harris, P. L., Olthof, T. and Terwogt, M. M. (1981). Children's knowledge of emotion. *Journal of Child Psychology and Psychiatry,* 22(3), 247-261.

Harter, S. (1977). A cognitive-developmental approach to children's expression of conflicting feelings and a technique to facilitate such expression in play therapy. *Journal of Consulting and Clinical Psychology,* 45(3), 417.

Hirshfeld-Becker, D. R. and Biederman, J. (2002). Rationale and principles for early intervention with young children at risk for anxiety disorders. *Clinical Child and Family Psychology Review,* 5(3), 161-172.

Hirshfeld-Becker, D. R., Masek, B., Henin, A., Blakely, L. R., Pollock-Wurman, R. A., McQuade, J., ... Rosenbaum, J. F. (2010). Cognitive behavioral therapy for 4-to 7-year-old children with anxiety disorders: a randomized clinical trial. *Journal of Consulting and Clinical Psychology,* 78(4), 498.

Hodges, K., Gordon, Y., and Lennon, M. P. (1990). Parent-Child Agreement on Symptoms Assessed via a Clinical Research Interview for Children: The Child Assessment Schedule (CAS). *Journal of Child Psychology and Psychiatry,* 31(3), 427-436. doi: 10.1111/j.1469-7610.1990.tb01579.x.

Hodges, K. and Saunders, W. (1989). Internal consistency of a diagnostic interview for children: The Child Assessment Schedule. *Journal of abnormal child psychology,* 17(6), 691-701.

Hodges, K., Saunders, W. B., Kashani, J., Hamlett, K., and Thompson, R. J. (1990). Internal Consistency of DSM-III Diagnoses Using the Symptom Scales of the Child Assessment Schedule. *Journal of the American Academy of Child and Adolescent Psychiatry,* 29(4), 635-641.

Hollingsworth, C. E., Tanguay, P. E., Grossman, L., and Pabst, P. (1981). Long-term outcome of obsessive-compulsive disorder in childhood. *Journal of the American Academy of Child Psychiatry,* 19(1), 134-144.

Izard, C. E. (1994). *Innate and universal facial expressions: evidence from developmental and cross-cultural research.*

Jersild, A. T. (1968). *Child psychology* (6th ed.). Englewood Cliffs, NJ: Prentice-Hall.

Kashdan, T. B. and Herbert, J. D. (2001). Social anxiety disorder in childhood and adolescence: Current status and future directions. *Clinical Child and Family Psychology Review,* 4(1), 37-61.

Kazdin, A. E. and Weisz, J. R. (1998). Identifying and developing empirically supported child and adolescent treatments. *Journal of consulting and clinical psychology,* 66(1), 19.

Keenan, K., Shaw, D. S., Walsh, B., Delliquadri, E., and Giovannelli, J. (1997). DSM-III-R Disorders in Preschool Children From Low-Income Families. *Journal of the American Academy of Child and Adolescent Psychiatry,* 36(5), 620-627.

Kendall, P. C. (1994). Treating anxiety disorders in children: Results of a randomized clinical trial. *Journal of Consulting and Clinical Psychology,* 62(1), 100-110. doi: 10.1037/0022-006x.62.1.100.

Kendall, P. C., Kane, M. and Howard, B. (1992). *Cognitivebehavioral therapy for anxious children: Therapist manual.*

Kennedy, S. J., Rapee, R. M. and Edwards, S. L. (2009). A selective intervention program for inhibited preschool-aged children of parents with an anxiety disorder: effects on current anxiety disorders and temperament. *Journal of the American Academy of Child and Adolescent Psychiatry,* 48 (6), 602-609.

King, N. J. and Gullone, E. (1990). Acceptability of fear reduction procedures with children. *Journal of Behavior Therapy and Experimental Psychiatry,* 21(1), 1-8. doi: http://dx.doi.org/10.1016/0005-7916(90)90042-J.

LaFreniere, P. J. and Capuano, F. (1997). Preventive intervention as means of clarifying direction of effects in socialization: Anxious-withdrawn preschoolers case. *Development and Psychopathology,* 9(3), 551-564.

Lagattuta, K. H., Sayfan, L. and Bamford, C. (2012). Do you know how I feel? Parents underestimate worry and overestimate optimism compared to child self-report. *Journal of Experimental Child Psychology,* 113(2), 211-232. doi: http://dx.doi.org/10.1016/j.jecp.2012.04.001.

Lavigne, J. V., LeBailly, S. A., Hopkins, J., Gouze, K. R., and Binns, H. J. (2009). The prevalence of ADHD, ODD, depression, and anxiety in a community sample of 4-year-olds. *Journal of Clinical Child and Adolescent Psychology,* 38(3), 315-328.

Macfarlane, J. W., Allen, L. and Honzik, M. P. (1954). A developmental study of the behavior problems of normal children between twenty-one months and fourteen years.

March, J., Foa, E., Gammon, P., Chrisman, A., Curry, J., Fitzgerald, D., ... Rynn, M. (2004). Cognitive-behavior therapy, sertraline, and their combination for children and adolescents with obsessive-compulsive disorder-The Pediatric OCD Treatment Study (POTS) randomized controlled trial. *Journal of the American Medical Association,* 292(16), 1969-1976.

March, J. and Mulle, K. (1998). *OCD in children and adolescents: A cognitive-behavioral treatment manual*: Guilford Press.

McCathie, H. and Spence, S. H. (1991). What is the revised fear survey schedule for children measuring? *Behaviour Research and Therapy,* 29(5), 495-502. doi: http://dx.doi.org/10.1016/0005-7967(91)90134-O.

McFarlane, A. C., Policansky, S. K. and Irwin, C. (1987). A longitudinal study of the psychological morbidity in children due to a natural disaster. *Psychological Medicine,* 17(03), 727-738.

Measelle, J. R., Ablow, J. C., Cowan, P. A., and Cowan, C. P. (1998). Assessing Young Children's Views of Their Academic, Social, and Emotional Lives: An Evaluation of the Self-Perception Scales of the Berkeley Puppet Interview. *Child development,* 69(6), 1556-1576.

Mian, N. D., Godoy, L., Briggs-Gowan, M. J., and Carter, A. S. (2012). Patterns of anxiety symptoms in toddlers and preschool-age children: Evidence of early differentiation. *Journal of anxiety disorders,* 26(1), 102-110.

Miller, L. C., Barrett, C. L. and Hampe, E. (1974). Phobias of childhood in a prescientific era.

Morris, R. J. and Kratochwill, T. R. (1983). *Treating children's fears and phobias: A behavioral approach* (Vol. 114): Cambridge Univ Press.

Muris, P., Meesters, C., Mayer, B., Bogie, N., Luijten, M., Geebelen, E., ... Smit, C. (2003). The Koala Fear Questionnaire: a standardized self-report scale for assessing fears and fearfulness in pre-school and primary school children. *Behaviour research and therapy,* 41(5), 597-617.

Murphy, D. M. (1985). Fears in preschool-age children. *Child care quarterly,* 14(3), 171-189.

Nannis, E. D. (1985). Structural Differences in Emotional Understanding and Their Application to Clinical Intervention.

Nannis, E. D. and Cowan, P. A. (1987). Emotional understanding: A matter of age, dimension, and point of view. *Journal of Applied Developmental Psychology,* 8(3), 289-304.

Ollendick, T. H. (1983). Reliability and validity of the revised fear survey schedule for children (FSSC-R). *Behaviour Research and Therapy,* 21(6), 685-692.

Ollendick, T. H., Grills, A. E. and King, N. J. (2001). Applying developmental theory to the assessment and treatment of childhood disorders: Does it make a difference? *Clinical Psychology and Psychotherapy,* 8(5), 304-314.

Ollendick, T. H. and King, N. J. (1998). Empirically supported treatments for children with phobic and anxiety disorders: Current status. *Journal of Clinical Child Psychology,* 27(2), 156-167.

Ollendick, T. H., King, N. J. and Chorpita, B. F. (2006). Empirically supported treatments for children and adolescents.

Ollendick, T. H., Öst, L.-G., Reuterskiöld, L., Costa, N., Cederlund, R., Sirbu, C., ... Jarrett, M. A. (2009). One-session treatment of specific phobias in youth: A randomized clinical trial in the United States and Sweden. *Journal of Consulting and Clinical Psychology,* 77(3), 504.

Öst, L.-G., Svensson, L., Hellström, K., and Lindwall, R. (2001). One-session treatment of specific phobias in youths: A randomized clinical trial. *Journal of Consulting and Clinical Psychology,* 69(5), 814.

Pediatric OCD. (2004). Treatment Study (POTS) Team. Cognitive-behavior therapy, sertraline, and their combination for children and adolescents with obsessive-compulsive disorder: the Pediatric OCD Treatment Study (POTS) randomized controlled trial. *Jama,* 292(16), 1969-1976.

Pincus, D. B., Eyberg, S. M. and Choate, M. L. (2005). Adapting parent-child interaction therapy for young children with separation anxiety disorder. *Education and treatment of children,* 28(2), 163-181.

Pincus, D. B., Santucci, L. C., Ehrenreich, J. T., and Eyberg, S. M. (2008). The implementation of modified parent-child interaction therapy for youth with separation anxiety disorder. *Cognitive and Behavioral Practice,* 15 (2), 118-125.

Pionek Stone, B., Kratochwill, T. R., Sladezcek, I., and Serlin, R. C. (2002). Treatment of selective mutism: A best-evidence synthesis. *School Psychology Quarterly,* 17(2), 168.

Rapee, R. M., Kennedy, S., Ingram, M., Edwards, S., and Sweeney, L. (2005). Prevention and early intervention of anxiety disorders in inhibited preschool children. *Journal of consulting and clinical psychology,* 73(3), 488.

Reich, W. (2000). Diagnostic interview for children and adolescents (DICA). *Journal of the American Academy of Child and Adolescent Psychiatry,* 39 (1), 59-66.

Richman, N., Stevenson, J. and Graham, P. (1975). Prevalence of behaviour problems in 3-year-old children: An epidemiological study in a London Borough. *Journal of Child Psychology and Psychiatry,* 16(4), 277-287.

Scahill, L., Riddle, M. A., McSwiggin-Hardin, M., Ort, S. I., King, R. A., Goodman, W. K., ... Leckman, J. F. (1997). Children's Yale-Brown obsessive compulsive scale: reliability and validity. *Journal of the American Academy of Child and Adolescent Psychiatry,* 36(6), 844-852.

Scheeringa, M. S. and Haslett, N. (2010). The reliability and criterion validity of the Diagnostic Infant and Preschool Assessment: a new diagnostic instrument for young children. *Child Psychiatry and Human Development,* 41(3), 299-312.

Scheeringa, M. S., Salloum, A., Arnberger, R. A., Weems, C. F., Amaya-Jackson, L., and Cohen, J. A. (2007). Feasibility and effectiveness of cognitive–behavioral therapy for posttraumatic stress disorder in preschool children: Two case reports. *Journal of Traumatic Stress,* 20(4), 631-636.

Scheeringa, M. S., Weems, C. F., Cohen, J. A., Amaya-Jackson, L., and Guthrie, D. (2011). Trauma-focused cognitive-behavioral therapy for posttraumatic stress disorder in three-through six year-old children: a randomized clinical trial. *Journal of Child Psychology and Psychiatry,* 52 (8), 853-860.

Scheeringa, M. S., Zeanah, C. H., Myers, L., and Putnam, F. W. (2005). Predictive validity in a prospective follow-up of PTSD in preschool children. *Journal of the American Academy of Child and Adolescent Psychiatry,* 44(9), 899-906.

Shaffer, D., Fisher, P., Lucas, C. P., Dulcan, M. K., and Schwab-Stone, M. E. (2000). NIMH Diagnostic Interview Schedule for Children Version IV (NIMH DISC-IV): description, differences from previous versions, and reliability of some common diagnoses. *Journal of the American Academy of Child and Adolescent Psychiatry,* 39(1), 28-38.

Shirk, S. R. (1988). *Cognitive development and child psychotherapy*: Plenum Press.

Shonkoff, J. P. and Phillips, D. A. (2000). *From neurons to neighborhoods: The science of early childhood development*: National Academies Press.

Silverman, W. K., Saavedra, L. M. and Pina, A. A. (2001). Test-Retest Reliability of Anxiety Symptoms and Diagnoses With the Anxiety Disorders Interview Schedule for DSM-IV: Child and Parent Versions. *Journal of the American Academy of Child and Adolescent Psychiatry,* 40 (8), 937-944.

Spence, S. H., Rapee, R., McDonald, C., and Ingram, M. (2001). The structure of anxiety symptoms among preschoolers. *Behaviour Research and Therapy,* 39(11), 1293-1316.

Stauffer, L. B. and Deblinger, E. (1996). Cognitive behavioral groups for nonoffending mothers and their young sexually abused children: A preliminary treatment outcome study. *Child Maltreatment,* 1(1), 65-76.

Sterba, S., Egger, H. L. and Angold, A. (2007). Diagnostic specificity and nonspecificity in the dimensions of preschool psychopathology. *Journal of Child Psychology and Psychiatry,* 48(10), 1005-1013.

Stewart, S., Geller, D., Jenike, M., Pauls, D., Shaw, D., Mullin, B., and Faraone, S. (2004). Long-term outcome of pediatric obsessive–compulsive disorder: a meta-analysis and qualitative review of the literature. *Acta Psychiatrica Scandinavica,* 110(1), 4-13.

Swedo, S. E., Rapoport, J. L., Leonard, H., Lenane, M., and Cheslow, D. (1989). Obsessive-compulsive disorder in children and adolescents: clinical phenomenology of 70 consecutive cases. *Archives of General Psychiatry,* 46(4), 335.

Tracey, S. A., Chorpita, B. F., Douban, J., and Barlow, D. H. (1997). Empirical evaluation of DSM-IV geralized anxiety disorder criteria in children and adolescents. *Journal of Clinical Child Psychology,* 26(4), 404-414.

Valla, J. P., Bergeron, L., Bidaut-Russell, M., St-Georges, M., and Gaudet, N. (1997). Reliability of the Dominic-R: A Young Child Mental Health Questionnaire Combining Visual and Auditory Stimuli. *Journal of Child Psychology and Psychiatry,* 38(6), 717-724.

Vasey, M. W., Crnic, K. A. and Carter, W. G. (1994). Worry in childhood: A developmental perspective. *Cognitive Therapy and Research,* 18(6), 529-549.

Verhulst, F., Althaus, M. and Berden, G. (1987). The Child Assessment Schedule: Parent-Child Agreement and Validity Measures. *Journal of Child Psychology and Psychiatry,* 28(3), 455-466.

Warren, S. L., Ollendick, T. H. and Simmens, S. J. (2008). Reliability and validity of the fear survey schedule for infants—preschoolers. *Depression and anxiety,* 25(12), E205-E207.

Waters, A. M., Ford, L. A., Wharton, T. A., and Cobham, V. E. (2009). Cognitive-behavioural therapy for young children with anxiety disorders: Comparison of a child+ parent condition versus a parent only condition. *Behaviour research and therapy,* 47(8), 654-662.

Welner, Z., Reich, W., Herjanic, B., Jung, K. G., and Amado, H. (1987). Reliability, validity, and parent-child agreement studies of the Diagnostic Interview for Children and Adolescents (DICA). *Journal of the American Academy of Child and Adolescent Psychiatry,* 26(5), 649-653.

Wood, J. J., Piacentini, J. C., Bergman, R. L., McCracken, J., and Barrios, V. (2002). Concurrent validity of the anxiety disorders section of the anxiety disorders interview schedule for DSM-IV: child and parent versions. *Journal of Clinical Child and Adolescent Psychology,* 31(3), 335-342.

In: Anxiety Disorders
Editor: Shiloh Angelus Roman
ISBN: 978-1-63117-392-9

Chapter 2

TOOLS AND METHODS FOR ANXIETY DISORDER ASSESSMENT AMONG CHILDREN AND ADOLESCENTS IN COGNITIVE AND BEHAVIORAL THERAPIES

***Rafika Zebdi, Ph.D.*[1,*] *and Salah Zebdi, M.D.*[2]**
[1]Senior Lecturer in Clinical Psychology, Laboratoire EVACLIPSY (EVAluation CLInique des troubles PSYchopathologiques et des PSYchothérapies, EA 4430),
Université Paris Ouest Nanterre La Défense, UFR SPSE, Nanterre, France
[2]Hospital Physician, Psychiatry, Head of Non-hospital Sector n.4, Hôpital Simone Veil, Montmorency, France

ABSTRACT

This chapter provides an overview of current knowledge on the assessment of anxiety disorders in children and adolescents in relation to CBT treatment.

Although the dimensional and categorical approaches have often been presented as opposed, today they appear to be compatible, particularly after the publication of version 5 of the Diagnostic and Statistical Manual of Mental Disorders (DSM-5), which overcomes this opposition and uses the two in combination. Nevertheless, a good working knowledge of these theoretical constructs is needed to choose

* E-mail: rzebdi@u-paris10.fr.

among the many available clinical tools, questionnaires, tests, etc. The abundance and variety of these instruments means that they need to be selected on a case-by-case basis. especially with children, with whom clinical methodology often requires the participation of an external informant (parent, other close adult).

Finally, despite the traditional division between the practices used in assessment and therapy, it is now possible, and even essential, to reconcile evaluative and therapeutic approaches on a single dynamic and longitudinal continuum.

Here, we examine this particular issue in the case of cognitive and behavioral therapies, wherein the role of the various instruments that we survey includes the assessment both of the treated psychopathologies and of the effectiveness of the therapies themselves.

We offer recommendations for the selection and use of clinical tools in screening and treatment for anxiety disorders in children and adolescents.

Keywords: Children, adolescents, assessment, anxiety disorders, cognitive and behavioral therapy

INTRODUCTION

Early assessment plays an essential role in the work of practitioners in child psychopathology, preceding any treatment. In the context of cognitive and behavioral therapies, forms of treatment with demonstrated effectiveness in anxiety disorders, assessment is an integral part of therapy—making it possible, on the one hand, to verify therapeutic results with single-case protocols, and, on the other hand, to verify the efficacy of a technique for a given pathology.

The objective of this chapter is to present a synthesis of knowledge on the assessment of anxiety disorders in children and adolescents and its relation to cognitive and behavioral therapies.

After a brief presentation of recent epidemiological data, we will examine two approaches that have classically been presented as antagonistic: dimensional and categorical. In the end, the two appear to be potentially compatible (notably with the publication of the new Diagnostic and Statistical Manual of Mental Disorders: DSM-5, American Psychiatric Association, 2013).

Clinicians and researchers need thorough knowledge of these theoretical constructs to make an appropriate choice among the available tools, since the different tools' development has been guided precisely by these approaches. They also correspond to two overall taxonomic approaches to the description of psychopathology: the clinical diagnostic approach and the quantitative empirical approach.

The two are jointly used in cognitive and behavioral therapies, since the therapeutic plan to be used will depend on the disorder presented (qualitative) and on the intensity of behavioral, cognitive and emotional manifestations (quantitative) as assessed at the beginning, in the middle, and at the end of treatment.

In the next section, we present assessment instruments that we consider relevant for practitioners working with children using cognitive and behavioral therapies, in an order that is designed to guide their choices. Given the multiplicity and variety of assessment instruments for anxiety disorders, clinicians facing the task of choosing among them often find themselves, understandably, lost. It is thus often necessary to take a case by case approach, particularly in children, where clinical methodology often requires the participation of an external informant (parent or other close adult).

Finally, despite the traditional divide between assessment and therapy, today it is possible—and even indispensable—to reconcile the two along a single dynamic and longitudinal continuum.

I. Epidemiological Data and the Evolving Conceptualization and Assessment of Anxiety Disorders in Children

Despite the high prevalence of anxiety disorders in children and adolescents, there are few extant studies on the topic (Costello, Mustillo, Erkanli, Keeler, and Angold, 2003; Chavira, Stein, Bailey, and Stein, 2004; Costello, Egger, and Angold, 2005; Muris and Broeren, 2009). Studies on these disorders in children often lump them together indiscriminately into a single category ("anxiety disorders"; Klein, 1994), despite the fact that they have been differentiated in adult psychopathology since the DSM-III (American Psychiatric Association, 1980). For example, to our knowledge the only studies on the French population were performed by Fombonne in 1992 and 1994, and look at the prevalence of psychopathological disturbances in general, in children between the ages of 8 and 11 years, as assessed using the Child Behavior Checklist (CBCL).

While the last two or three decades have seen a number of publications on certain specific anxiety syndromes, such as posttraumatic stress disorder, obsessive-compulsive disorder, social phobia and multiple anxiety disorders, researchers have neglected other anxiety disorders such as panic disorder-agoraphobia, specific phobia, separation anxiety and generalized anxiety disorder (Muris and Broeren, 2009). This phenomenon is probably due to the fact that fear and anxiety are considered to be normal phenomena, which are part of child development (Muris and Broeren, 2009). As Jan Costello and colleagues (2005) emphasized, direct assessment of young children is difficult because of their cognitive immaturity. Children need a minimum of cognitive and communicative skills to be able to talk about their worries, their fear or their panic attacks.

Recent studies, however, have given evidence of such disturbances in preschool-age children (Costello et al., 2003), highlighting the need to precisely differentiate these early anxious symptoms. Generalized anxiety disorder (GAD) seems to appear around the age of 6 years (Costello et al., 2005), and half of children between the ages of 7 and 10 years who are diagnosed with an anxiety disorder fulfill the DSM diagnostic criteria for GAD (Layne, Bernat, Victor, and Bernstein, 2009). More generally, this disorder is found in more than 10% of children and adolescents, with a mean age of onset of 8.5 years, and higher prevalence in girls (Lewinsohn, Gotlib, Lewinsohn, Seeley and Allen, 1998; Keeton, Kolos, and Walcup, 2009). Doerfler, Toscano and Connor (2008) showed that children suffering from comorbid separation anxiety and panic disorder presented the disorder at a mean age of 6.9 years (SD=3.3).

Goodwin and Gotlib (2004) found that the prevalence of panic disorder in their population was 3.3%, and Diler, Birmaher, Brent, Axelson, Firinciogullari et al. (2004), in a study on a large clinical sample, found that approximately 2% of patients presented a panic disorder, and that most of these were female, "Caucasian," and adolescent.

Social phobia was long assumed to be rare in children, since it was considered normal for children to be shy, but recent results have shown that it is relatively common, starting at the age of 11 years (Essau, Conradt, and Peterman, 1999; Gren-Landell, Tillfors, Furmark et al., 2009; Rao, Beidel, Turner et al., 2007; Ranta, Kaltiala-Heino, Rantanen, and Marttunen, 2009; Van Roy, Kristensen, Groholt, and Clench-Aas, 2009).

Recent progress in research on anxiety has led researchers such as Klein (2009) to question the appropriateness of grouping together all symptoms linked to anxiety under a single label as "anxiety disorders."

II. The Place of the Categorical and Dimensional Approaches in the Assessment of Anxiety Disorders

Along with changes in the conceptualization of anxiety disorders, recent years have seen profound changes in psychometric instruments for the assessment of anxiety. In the 1980s and 1990s, most measures of anxiety were structured interviews that were well-adapted, but particularly time-consuming. They were designed for the diagnosis of specific anxiety disorders. There were also self-administered general questionnaires, measuring the overall level of anxiety without pinpointing the nature of the anxiety presented or making it possible to diagnose the corresponding anxiety disorder.

Moreover, for many years, two distinct approaches to psychopathological disorders have coexisted and sometimes been opposed to one another: the traditional categorical approach and the quantitative dimensional approach.

The categorical approach has been used in the majority of cases. This approach refers to diagnostic entities whose limits are precisely defined using inclusion and exclusion criteria. Although the categorical approach is relatively reliable, it is not sufficient to give an account of the quantitative aspects of anxiety pathologies, and the variability or intensity of the manifestations encountered in clinical practice.

The categorical diagnostic system inherited from Kraepelin (1856-1926), and exemplified recently in the DSM-IV and the ICD 10, consists in diagnosing disorders in all-or-nothing fashion (present/absent). These classification systems are based on a "top-down" approach (Figure 1; Chahed, 2010): that is, they start from psychopathological categories made up of symptoms defined and validated by a panel of experts. The experts collect semiological information on the basis of standardized interviews, allowing them to define the required symptoms for each disorder (diagnostic category; Achenbach, 1991; Achenbach and Rescorla, 2001).

It was not until the 1980s that the diagnostic categories of child psychopathology began to be added to the DSM and the ICD, and since then they have been in constant evolution. The nosography of international classification systems whose aim is to rationalize the diagnostic process in psychiatry has evolved, notably that of anxiety disorders in children. The penultimate version of the DSM (IV-TR, 2000) emphasized the commonalities between child, adolescent and adult anxiety disorders, connecting, for example, hyper-anxiety and generalized anxiety.

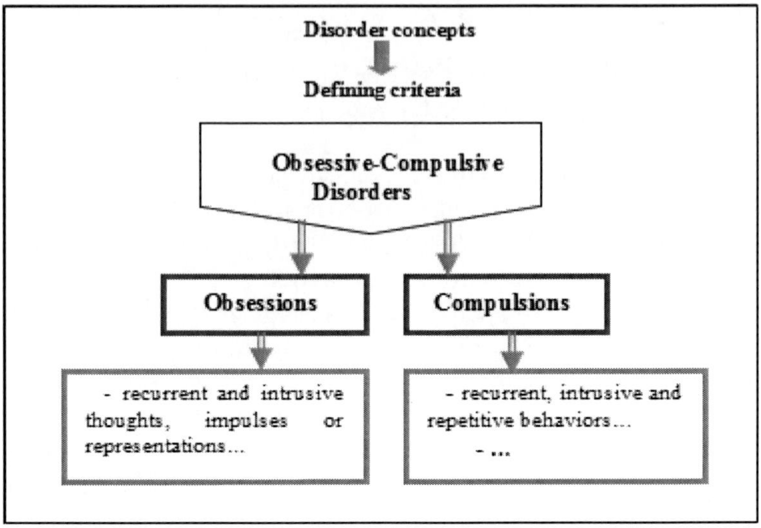

Figure 1. The Top-Down Approach (Chahed, 2010; Krueger, 2002; Achenbach and Rescorla, 2001).

The aim of this decision, which was based on the results of field studies, was to facilitate the identification of links between anxiety disorders at different ages and more clearly characterize their life-course trajectories.

However, these categories cannot be used to track the whole set of clinical manifestations observed on daily basis in a sufficiently precise and powerful fashion. On the contrary, there exist clinical situations of manifest suffering, in terms of the number and intensity of symptoms, which nevertheless are not sufficient to make a categorical diagnosis. In other words, the categorical approach would neglect a child who presents five symptoms where six are needed to validate the diagnosis, while the dimensional approach identifies the child as having subclinical symptomatology, and distinguishes the child from one who presents none of the symptoms of the disorder.

Notably for these reasons, the dimensional approach is now widely used, both in clinical and research contexts, due to its suitability for capturing such distinctions and its precision in fine descriptions of psychopathological disorders, another area where the categorical model shows its limitations.

The dimensional approach is based on a hierarchical model (Krueger, 2002) which consists in statistically identifying the signs that are frequently associated to one another in a given population, thereby constituting syndromic groups.

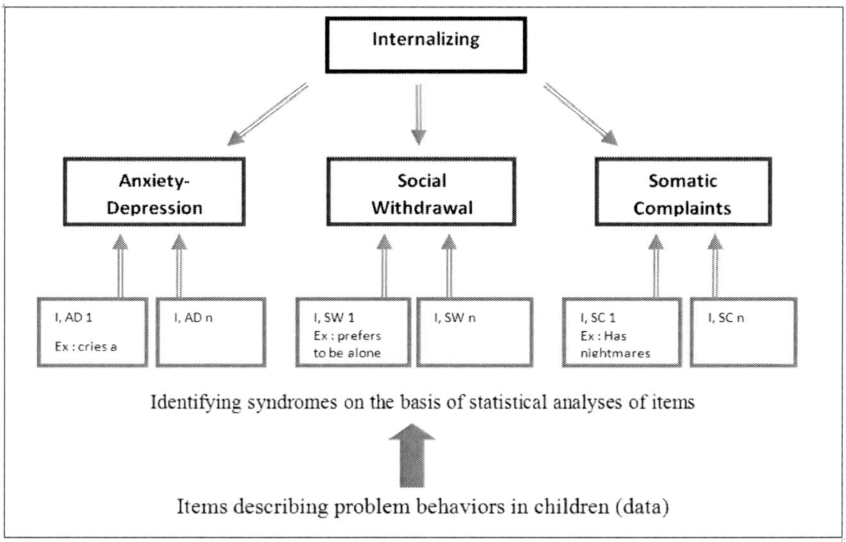

Legend: I= Internalizing; AD=Anxiety/Depression; SW=Social Withdrawal [Replaces RI]; SC = Somatic Complaints [Replaces PS]; n = other items.

Figure 2. Principle of the Bottom-Up Approach (Chahed, 2010; Achenbach 1991; Achenbach and Rescorla, 2001).

This is also known as the "bottom-up" model, as illustrated by Figure 2 (Chahed, 2010), which is inspired by those of Krueger (2002) and Achenbach and Rescorla (2001). It offers a good illustration of the logic of the construction of assessment instruments under a dimensional model.

A certain number of psychometric instruments have been developed on the basis of the dimensional approach, with the advantage of being usable in both self- and proxy assessment, which increases the number of information sources on clinical situations, enriching their assessment. This is true of the ASEBA (Achenbach System of Empirically Based Assessment) instruments developed by Thomas Achenbach starting in the 1960s (1978, 1981, 1991, 2001), one of the precursors of the dimensional approach, which can be used to perform statistical comparisons between the scores obtained by three assessors (the child with the Youth Self-Report, the parent with the Child Behavior Checklist, and the teacher with the Teacher Report Form) and also to compare them to norms obtained from very large samples. Moreover, Achenbach and Rescorla (2001) integrated DSM-oriented scales into such instruments in order to suggest the possibility of diagnosing certain disorders according to DSM-IV criteria.

III. Toward a New Nosological Conception that Combines the Two Approaches

Transformations in this domain had already started in the middle of the 1960s, with the development and application of the dimensional approach, based on measurements of the intensity of anxiety phenomena independently of any particular diagnostic framework.

More and more authors are highlighting the view that in the practice of child psychopathology, standardized dimensional measurements are highly useful, or even a requirement. Hudziak, Achenbach, Althoff and Pine (2007), for example, explained that multiple sources of information are needed to assess psychopathological disorders in children, since children cannot always totally describe their disturbances due to their cognitive and linguistic immaturity. But the low level of agreement between informants makes it difficult to categorize children as "sick" or "healthy" (Verhulst and Van der Ende, 1992), and categorical measurements only rarely integrate several information sources. Brown and Barlow (2009), who studied disagreements between informants on anxiety disorder diagnoses, found that these disagreements pertain mainly to diagnoses of social phobia, specific phobia and obsessive-compulsive disorder. In many of these cases, one informant describes a clinical level of symptoms while the other describes a subclinical level.

Van Oort, Greaves-Lord, Verhulst, Ormel and Huizink (2009) highlighted the need for a complementary classification system that includes both approaches, and subscribed to the idea of integrating a quantitative axis into the DSM-5 in order to integrate a dimensional perspective. They argued that this would help clinicians and researchers not only to assess the presence or absence of a pathology, but also its degree of manifestation. Like Hudziak, Achenbach et al. (2007), these authors emphasized the possibility of adding thresholds to dimensional instruments in order to facilitate yes/no diagnostics for the purpose of therapeutic decisions. The dimensional axis also offers the possibility of using instruments that are less time-consuming, can be offered in a multiple-informants version, and provide quantitative indices of variation in symptoms and normative behaviors by age and sex.

In Figure 3 we have attempted to illustrate the perspective that integrates the principles of the two approaches. The idea is to picture the categorical approach as a "ruler" along which a cursor can move according to the number of symptoms present.

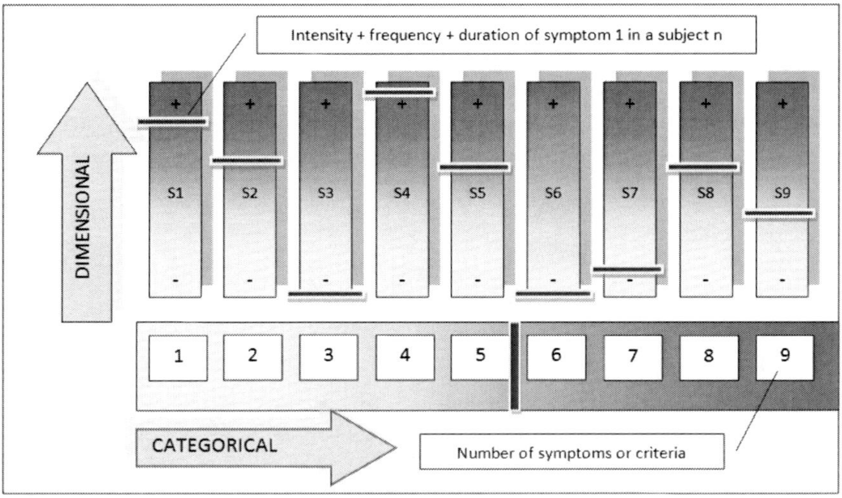

(Zebdi, 2011 ©).

Figure 3. Representation of categorical and dimensional approaches to the symptoms of psychopathological disorders.

When this cursor surpasses a precise number of symptoms (here, five), this indicates a positive diagnosis of the disorder. Simultaneously, the dimensional approach (at the top of the figure) can be used to specify the intensity and/or the frequency and/or the duration (according to the type of validation of the criterion) of each symptom present (here, symptoms S1, S2, S4, S5 and S8 present an intensity and/or frequency and/or duration which classifies them as pathological).

It is evident today, notably after the publication of the DSM-5, that the dimensional and categorical approaches, which have classically been considered distinct, are becoming potentially compatible and jointly usable in assessment and therapy.

IV. Instruments for the Assessment of Anxiety Disorders in Children

The dimensional approach has driven the development of instruments that are faster to use, that can be filled in by either children or parents, and that permit a more precise assessment of the various anxiety disorders and/or the diagnosis of specific disorders. Among these instruments, we will cite a certain number of questionnaires and inventories for the general assessment of anxiety, others that can be used for a more specific assessment of anxiety disorders (some of which possess parallel forms) and that permit the collection of data from multiple informants, as well as instruments which are particularly useful in the context of cognitive and behavioral therapy.

1. General Assessment

In the first section, we will present three general assessment instruments: the Child Behavior Checklist (CBCL) and its parallel form the Youth Self-Report (YSR), as well as the Strengths and Difficulties Questionnaire—self-report and teacher-/parent-completed versions (SDQ).

ASEBA: Achenbach System Empirically Based Assessment Inventories

The CBCL, a form to be filled in by the parents of children and adolescents between the ages of 6-18 years (Achenbach and Rescorla, 2001), and the YSR, a self-assessment form for children and adolescents between the ages of 11 and 18 years (Achenbach and Rescorla, 2001) were developed in 1978 by Thomas Achenbach, in the United States. Their objective is to provide a standardized description of the behavior and emotional disturbances of children between the ages of 6 and 18 years (Achenbach and Rescorla, 2001), as well as their skills. This relatively long reference period, at the scale of the child, can be used to establish the occurrence of infrequent psychopathological manifestations or to establish their duration.

The CBCL and the YSR have been translated into more than 85 languages. According to Gladman and Lancaster (2003), these scales practically have a monopoly in the domain of the assessment of children's adaptive functioning. The advertised time required to complete them is an average of 15 to 20 minutes for the American version; experience has shown that in clinical samples, 30 to 45 minutes are required for each form (Zebdi and Petot, 2013).

For the CBCL, the information source is one of the parents (the child's father or mother, or the two together), or any other person who knows the child well (parental substitute, educator, etc.). The YSR is completed by the child or adolescent (starting at age 11). The CBCL and the YSR are made up of two sections. The first part is made up of open questions, bearing on adaptive behaviors in the daily life of the child or adolescent, their social relationships, and their school performance. All these behaviors are grouped together under the heading "social skills" in the form of three scales: Activities, Social and School. The results of these scales are rarely used in international studies, even though they are of clear interest for the assessment of the impact of pathology, and notably anxious pathology, on the three targeted domains.

The second part, which is more widely used in research, assesses either the presence or absence, or the frequency and intensity of several pathological behaviors on the basis of 98 common problem-items (cross-informant) and thirty specific items grouped into eight syndromic scales. These scales relate to the presence or absence of the following syndromes: 1) Social Withdrawal; 2) Somatic Complaints; 3) Anxiety/Depression; 4) Interpersonal Problems; 5) Thought Problems; 6) Attention-Hyperactivity Problems; 7) Delinquency and 8) Aggressive Behaviors.

Certain syndromic scales are grouped into two broader dimensions: Internalizing and Externalizing, depending on whether affective/emotional disturbances or behavioral disturbances predominate. The first three syndromes (Social Withdrawal, Somatic Complaints, and Anxiety/Depression) make up the Internalizing scale. The two last syndromes (Delinquency, Aggressive Behaviors) make up the Externalizing scale. Note that this dichotomy is classically found in all research instruments in child psychopathology (Fombonne et al., 1988).

The CBCL and the YSR also include eight "DSM-Oriented Scales" which are designed to establish a profile with a certain diagnostic correspondence to the DSM: Affective Problems, Anxiety Problems, Somatic Problems, Attention Deficit-Hyperactivity Problems, Oppositional Defiant Problems, Conduct Problems, Obsessive-Compulsive Problems and Posttraumatic Stress Problems. The scores obtained on each dimension, as reported by the various respondents, can be compared to the clinical thresholds established by Achenbach. These clinical thresholds vary according to age, sex and informant. In order to obtain an index of the disturbance of the child or the adolescent, the author recommends comparing their score to age- and sex-adapted clinical thresholds. Since the 1990s, Achenbach and Rescorla (1992; 2000) have also developed a form of the CBCL for preschool-age children (1.5-5 years).

In the case of anxiety disorders, the results on overall scales (Total Problems score, Internalizing score, and Externalizing score), on anxiety-related syndromic scales (Anxiety/Depression, Social Withdrawal, and Somatic Complaints), as well as on the DSM-Oriented Scales for Affective Problems, Anxiety Problems, Somatic Problems, Obsessive-Compulsive

Problems and Posttraumatic Stress Problems can act as very good indicators of the presence of anxious symptoms and as a first-line assessment to precede a more specific assessment, if necessary.

The Strengths and Difficulties Questionnaire

Another similar instrument is The Strengths and Difficulties Questionnaire (SDQ; Goodman, 2001). There are two nearly identical versions to be completed by the parents or teacher of children between the ages of 3 and 16 years, or by children/adolescents between the ages of 11-16 years themselves (Goodman, 1997; Goodman et al., 1998). It offers a succinct measure of prosocial behavior, psychopathologies, and psychological adjustment in young people.

There are more than 40 translations of this instrument, which is made up of 25 propositions, some positive and others negative. Responses are given on a three-point Likert scale, indicating the extent to which each proposition applies to the child.

The 25 items are divided among five scales of five items each, generating scores for 1) emotional symptoms, 2) conduct problems, 3) hyperactivity/inattention, 4) peer relationship problems, and 5) prosocial behavior (Goodman, 2001). The selection of items on the SDQ and their grouping into scales were based on contemporary nosological concepts (the subscales can be mapped onto DSM-IV criteria) as well as on factorial analyses (Goodman, 2001). The questionnaire has demonstrated good reliability and validity, and can be used to precisely determine the presence of psychiatric diagnoses (Goodman, Ford, Simmons, Gatward and Meltzer, 2003).

In many cases, the SDQ works at least as well as the Achenbach questionnaire (1991), with numerous correlations between the two (Goodman and Scott, 1999; Klasen et al., 2000; Koskelainen et al., 2000). Cross-correlations are higher than is usually found for other questionnaires of the same type (Goodman et al., 1998), perhaps reflecting the close similarity of the questionnaires administered to multiple informants (children and parents or teachers).

Both the CBCL and the SDQ also offer an initial baseline before the beginning of cognitive and behavioral therapy, and can be used as instruments to measure the effectiveness of therapy for anxious symptoms and to visualize the improvement of the child's state in various domains. With the parallel forms, they can also be used to assess the perception of the adults around the child of the changes brought about by therapy.

2. Specific Anxiety Disorder Assessment Instruments

Recent years have seen considerable development in instruments for the assessment of specific anxiety disorders. Given their abundance, it can be difficult to navigate among them. Differences in the methods, samples and ages of the children in studies that use these various tools can also make comparison between their findings difficult. Examples include:

- the Social Phobia and Anxiety Inventory for Children (SPAI-C; Beidel, Turner, and Morris, 1995, 2000),
- the Multidimensional Anxiety Scale for Children (MASC; March, 1997),
- the Children's Moods, Fears and Worries Questionnaire (CMFWQ; Bayer, Sansan, and Hemphill, 2006),
- the Preschool Anxiety Scale (PAS; Spence et al., 2001),
- the Pediatric Anxiety Rating Scale (PARS; Research Unit on Pediatric Psychopharmacology Anxiety Study Group, 2002),
- Screen for Child Anxiety Related Emotional Disorders (SCARED; Birmaher et al., 1997, 1999), and
- the Spence Children's Anxiety Scale (SCAS; Spence, 1997).

We have decided to present the last two instruments in this list in particular, since they each include two versions, one for parents and one for the children themselves. As we mentioned in the introduction, this multiple-informants approach is very important in the assessment of psychopathological disorders in children, since a minimum of cognitive and communicative skills are needed for children to be able to talk about their worries, fear, or panic attacks. Assessment by a parent or another adult who is close to the child is thus needed to provide complementary information.

Moreover, the SCARED and the SCAS were specially created to aid in the diagnosis of specific anxiety disorders that are usually neglected and under-diagnosed, like generalized anxiety disorder (GAD), panic disorder (PD) and social phobia (SP). The subscales of these two instruments correspond to the categories of anxiety disorders in the DSM, and the items that constitute them refer to its criteria. Moreover, the SCARED was particularly conceived to detect anxiety disorders in children that have usually been under-diagnosed and under-treated due to their comorbidity with other psychiatric disorders, which could mask the presence of an underlying anxiety (Birmaher et al., 1999).

The Screen for Child Anxiety Related Emotional Disorders (SCARED)

The SCARED was initially developed by Birmaher, Khetarpal, Brent et al. (1997), who administered an 85-item questionnaire to 341 children and adolescents from the general population (SCARED-C) and to 300 parents (SCARED-P).

Factorial analyses of the two versions produced five factors: panic/somatic, generalized anxiety, separation anxiety, social phobia, and school phobia. After these analyses, the original scale was reduced to 38 items.

This study was reproduced with a new sample of 180 children and adolescents from the general population along with 166 parents. For this reproduction, 3 items were added to the social phobia scale; this version of the SCARED thus included 41 items. The reproduction confirmed the five-factor structure and psychometric properties of the SCARED, which has subsequently been used in numerous studies with clinical samples of American children and adolescents presenting anxiety and/or affective disorders (Monga, Birmaher, Chiapetta, Brent et al., 2000; Wren, Bridge, and Birmaher, 2004; Wren, Berg, Heiden et al., 2007).

To our knowledge, the only non-clinical sample studied in the United States was a sample of young African Americans (*N*=111) recruited in an urban parochial school (Boyd, Ginsburg, Lambert et al., 2003). The SCARED was subsequently translated and adapted in several European countries: the Netherlands (Hale III, Raajmakers, Muris, and Meeus, 2005, 2008), the Dutch-speaking part of Belgium (Muris, Merckelbach, Ollendick and al, 2002), Germany (Essau, Muris, and Ederer, 2002), Italy (Crocetti, HaleIII, Fermani, Raajmakers, and Meeus, 2009), and Spain (Vigil-Colet, Canals, Cosi et al., 2009).

In all of these validity studies, the child version of the questionnaire (SCARED-C) was used, and the participants were recruited in schools. These studies reproduced the five-factor structure of the original American version, except for the German study where a principal components analysis identified six eigenvectors, dividing the separation anxiety scale into two different scales: "separation fear" and "worry about harm" (Essau et al., 2002). A Chinese study that used the child and parent questionnaires also replicated the five-factor structure for the two versions (Su, Wang, Fan, Su, and Gao, 2008), which demonstrates the robustness of this factorial structure beyond Western population samples.

Collectively, these studies gave evidence of variations linked to cultural differences, with a total score running from 11.46 (Netherlands) to 19.46 (African Americans) and very similar standard deviations between 10.69

(Italy) and 12.6 (Belgium). As expected, these values are lower than those found in American studies on children and adolescents suffering from anxiety disorders, e.g., 26.0 (SD=14.8, in Monga et al., 2000) or 35.1 (SD=17.3, in Birmaher et al., 1999). The same sex- and age-related differences were found in almost all the samples taken from the general population. Girls score significantly higher than boys on all scales, with one exception, school anxiety (Crocetti et al., 2009; Hale, Crocetti et al., 2011). In all countries, the scores of both sexes increase with age on all scales except the separation anxiety scale, where they decrease in a stable fashion in all cultures.

The Spence Children's Anxiety Scale (SCAS)

Developed by Spence in 1997, the objective of the SCAS is to assess the symptoms of anxiety disorders in children and adolescents between the ages of 7 and 19 years. The first questionnaire, consisting of 44 items (38 assessing anxiety disorders and 6 items on a subscale intended to reduce the bias toward negative responding) were administered to 698 children between the ages of 8 and 12 years. Factorial analyses identified six factors: Panic attacks and agoraphobia, generalized anxiety and overanxious disorder, separation anxiety, social phobia, fears of physical injury, and obsessive-compulsive disorder.

This study was reproduced with a new sample of 2,052 children and adolescents from the Australian general population (Spence, 1998). The reproduction confirmed the six-factor structure and the psychometric properties of the SCAS, which has since been used in numerous studies with samples of children and adolescents both from the general population and with anxiety and/or affective disorders (Whiteside and Brown, 2008; Nauta et al., 2004; Muris, Merckelbach et al., 2002; Muris et al., 2000; Spence, 1998).

The SCAS has also been translated and adapted in a number of other countries: the Netherlands (Muris, Schmidt, and Merckelbach, 2000), Japan (Essau et al., 2004; Ishikawa, Sato, and Sasagawa, 2009), Germany (Essau et al., 2004; Essau, Muris, and Ederer, 2002), Greece (Mellon and Moutavelis, 2007), Spain (Tortella-Feliu,Balle, Servera, and de la Banda, 2005), China (Essau, Leung, Conradt, Cheng, and Wong, 2008), South Africa (Muris, Schmidt, Engelbrecht, and Perold, 2002), and the United States (Whiteside and Brown, 2008).

A study by Muris et al. (2000) on a sample of 1,011 children between the ages of 7 and 19 years demonstrated good convergent validity between the SCARED and the SCAS. They found a strong correlation between total scores on the two questionnaires (0.89) and satisfactory correlations between the scales for particular pathologies (between 0.63 and 0.79).

Both the SCAS and the SCARED are excellent first-line tools, which can be used both to assess overall anxiety levels and to determine the nature of the child's anxiety.

This second point is essential for appropriate therapeutic orientation. Therapeutic approaches to social phobia are not the same as those to separation anxiety syndromes, for example.

The other advantage of these inventories is that the scores can be used as a baseline in evaluating a cognitive and behavioral therapy from the point of view of both child and parents. They thus avoid the accumulation of inventories at different stages of care, which seldom allow comparison between results at different times before, during and after therapy.

3. Useful Assessment Instruments for Cognitive and Behavioral Therapy

In this section we will present a number of questionnaires that are of particular interest in the context of cognitive and behavioral therapy. The instruments presented above are also quite appropriate for use in the context of such therapies, but the added value of these instruments lies in the content of the items.

L'Echelle Comportementale d'Anxiété and Phobie (Behavioral Anxiety and Phobia Scale)

The Behavioral Anxiety and Phobia Scale (ECAP; Vera, 1996) is intended to assess the fears expressed by children and adolescents between the ages of 8 and 18 years in several domains of daily activity (social, family, school and self-image).

This questionnaire offers a measure of the intensity of various fears: school phobia, social phobia, fear of illness, separation anxiety and simple phobia. The ECAP is made up of two scales: a fears scale (76 items) and a phobic avoidance scale (21 items). Completion time is around 15 minutes, with responses on a three-point Likert scale from 1 (Almost never) to 3 (Often). It yields a total fear intensity score and a total score for the intensity or frequency of phobic avoidance. This tool has good psychometric properties (sensitivity, reliability and validity).

A feature of this scale that is of particular interest is the set of three major anxiety-producing themes embedded within it, as identified by factorial analyses:

1) Factor I: Self-image, skills and personal success (27 items). These items relate to the fear of not succeeding, the fear that one's social image will be criticized (apprehensions which concern both school and social domains). This factor can be interpreted as the fear of not having sufficient skills for personal success.
2) Factor II: Peer group interaction (14 items). These items relate to the fear of interaction with the peer group in a formal context (school, club, etc.).
3) Factor III: Fear of dangers threatening the child's own physical integrity or that of the child's parents (19 items). These items can be interpreted as the fear of separation or disruption of the relationship with an attachment figure.

The ECAP has been tested on a French population (Vera, 1996), but unfortunately has not yet been exported. It would be of interest to adapt and validate it in other languages and for other general and clinical populations.

The Children's Automatic Thoughts Scale (CATS)

The Children's Automatic Thoughts Scale (CATS, Schniering and Rapee, 2002) is a general measurement tool for negative self-descriptions, sometimes through externalizing and internalizing problems. The CATS is not the only instrument for assessing automatic negative thoughts in children. There are others, such as the Automatic Thoughts Questionnaire for Children (ATQ-C; Stark, Best and Adam, 1990), the Cognition Checklist (CCL; Beck, Brown, Steer, Eidelson, and Riskind 1987), and the Cognitive Triad Inventory for Children (CTI-C; Kaslow, Stark, Printz, Livingston, and Tsai, 1992). But the CATS is one of the few measures that was not created by adapting an instrument originally designed for adults. This practice has been criticized since it was shown that children's understanding of items on self-assessment measures could sometimes differ substantially from that of adults (Campbell, Rapee and Spence 2001; Schniering, Hudson and Rapee 2000). The development of the CATS is based on a preceding study that used an exhaustive analysis of negative self-descriptions by children and adolescents to generate items that are sensitive to developmental change (Schniering and Rapee, 2002). Children and adolescents were asked to rate the frequency with which they had had each thought over the course of the preceding week, on a five-point scale from "not at all" to "all the time." The items were divided into four separate subscales on cognitive contents relating to physical threats, social threats, personal failure and hostility. The ratings between 0 and 4 for each item are added together to produce the total score, with high results reflecting a greater frequency of automatic negative thoughts. This measure has good psychometric properties, and each of the subscales relates to a different form of child psychopathology, including anxiety, depression and externalizing problems (Schniering and Rapee, 2002, 2004a, 2004b). The study of Schniering and Lyneham (2007) on 891 children between the ages of 7 and 17 years with a principal diagnosis of anxiety disorder showed that the CATS is extremely sensitive to changes produced by cognitive-behavioral therapies that are focused on internalizing symptoms, but not externalizing symptoms.

There was a significant decrease in the frequency of negative thoughts about social threat, physical threat and personal failure compared to the control group (subjects on the waiting list).

The Cognitive Avoidance Questionnaire (CAQ)

The CAQ is a questionnaire developed and validated with adults and adolescents by Gosselin and colleagues in 2002. It is composed of 25 items. A principal components analysis revealed a component structure considered to reflect five different avoidance strategies (five items per component): 1) distraction, 2) avoidance of stimuli that trigger intrusive thoughts, 3) thought suppression, 4) thought substitution and 5) transformation of mental images into verbal thoughts.

A certain number of psychopathological disorders, and anxiety and mood disorders in particular, are characterized by the presence of recurring and persistent cognitive intrusions (e.g., worries, obsessions, doubts, etc.). When such thoughts occur, they produce discomfort. This leads to the adoption of strategies to avoid them or drive them out of the mind. These avoidance behaviors are thought to play a role in the etiology, development and maintenance of a number of psychopathological disorders, such as GAD, OCD and specific phobias. Deliberate suppression leads to a paradoxical effect which manifests itself through an increase in the frequency of the thoughts in question, since, by preventing exposure to the disturbing thoughts and thus the emotional process of habituation, a pattern that several authors, such as Clark, have called a "rebound effect" (Clark, Ball and Pape, 1991; Clark, Winton and Thynn, 1993; Lavy and van den Hout, 1990). This questionnaire provides clinicians with a useful instrument for assessing cognitive avoidance in adolescents between the ages of 12 and 19 years. The CAQ and its five subscales have excellent internal coherence, satisfactory validity and very good temporal stability.

L'Inventaire de Schéma Précoces pour Enfants (Inventory of Early Schemas for Children; ISPE)

The ISPE is an inventory that was created by Rusinek and Hautekeete (1999), who based it on Young's (1990, 1991) questionnaires on early maladaptive schemas for adults. This questionnaire, adapted from the abridged version created by Schmidt and colleagues (1995), is aimed at children between the ages of 11 and 15 years. Thirteen schemas are assessed in total: 1) Incompetence/inferiority, 2) emotional deprivation, 3) isolation, 4) insufficient self-control, 5) mistrust, 6) self-sacrifice, 7) unrelenting moral standards, 8) abandonment, 9) attachment, 10) vulnerability, 11) dependency, 12) emotional inhibition and 13) fear of losing control. It is intended to identify the early maladaptive schemas of children suffering from personality disorders.

It includes twenty-six distinct items, two questions for each schema. These items are affirmations that children respond to on a three-point scale according to their level of acceptance. In a therapeutic context, as suggested by Young and Klosko (1993), this identification of early maladaptive schemas can be used to devise a plan for cognitive restructuring to reduce their activity. Such schemas can induce interpretation biases that may be involved in causing and maintaining certain psychopathological disorders, notably anxiety disorders.

Other Questionnaires and Scales

In Table 1 we present several other assessment questionnaires used with children and adolescents, notably in the framework of cognitive and behavioral therapies.

The four instruments presented in Table 1 have the advantage of containing subscales that can aid in assessing certain behaviors or attitudes, and thus to better choose the techniques to be applied, and at the same time to assess their efficacy, such as for example behavioral avoidance with the CAM, or the physiological symptoms of anxiety with the RCMAS or the MASC.

There are a good number of other instruments aimed at assessing specific anxiety disorders, and while it would be difficult to present an exhaustive list here, in Table 2 we present those that we see as useful for the assessment of specific anxiety disorders. Most of these questionnaires were presented by Bouvard and Cottraux (2005), Bouvard (2008) and Vera (2009).Ultimately, despite the traditional divide between the practices of assessment and therapy, today it seems possible to reconcile evaluative and therapeutic approaches in a dynamic and longitudinal continuum, notably thanks to the instruments presented in this chapter, which have become a necessity.

Table 1. General Assessment Questionnaires Used in CBT

Instrument	Measure	Assessed factors/ dimensions	Age	Form(s)
Multidimensional Anxiety Scale for Children (MASC; March, 1997; March et al., 1997)	Anxiety	5 factors Physical symptoms Harm avoidance Social anxiety Separation anxiety Anxiety Index Subscale	8 to 18 years	Self-assessment
Child Avoidance Measure-Self Report and Parent Report (CAMS / CAMP; Whiteside et al., 2013)	Avoidance	1 factor Child's tendency to avoid stimuli that elicit anxiety fear or worry	7 to 18 years	Self-assessment Proxy assessment
State-Trait Anxiety Inventory for Children (STAIC; Spielberger,1973)	Anxiety	2 factors Generalized anxiety (trait) Anxiety at the moment of assessment (state)	9 to 12 years	Self-assessment
Revised Children's Manifest Anxiety Scale (RCMAS; Reynolds & Richmond, 1985)	Anxiety	5 factors Physical anxiety symptoms Concentration Worry/oversensitivity Social desirability Denial of undesirable behaviors	8 to 19 years	Self-assessment

Table 2. Specific Assessment Questionnaires Used in CBT

Anxiety disorder	Questionnaire	Measure	Factors	Age	Form(s)
Social phobia	Social Anxiety Scale for Children Revised (SASCR; La Greca & Stone, 1993) Social Anxiety Scale for Adolescents (SAS-A; La Greca & Lopez, 1998)	Social anxiety	Fear of Negative Evaluation Social Avoidance and Distress with new or unfamiliar people Social avoidance and distress, generalized	8 to 18 years	Self-assessment Proxy assessment
	Social Cognitions Questionnaire (SCQ; Wells, Stopa & Clark, 1993)	Automatic thoughts related to social anxiety	Negative self-concept Anticipation of performance failure Anticipation of negative evaluation by others	12 to 18 years	Self-assessment
Obsessive-Compulsive Disorders	Children's Yale-Brown Obsessive Compulsive Scale (CY-BOCS; Storch, 2006)	Obsessions and Compulsions	Obsessions Compulsions	8 to 17 years	Self-assessment Proxy assessment (parent or clinician following interview with parent/child)
	Leyton Obsessional Inventory-Child Version (LOI-CV, Berg et al., 1985;1988)	Obsessions	Obsessions	8 to 18 years	Self-assessment
	Yale Children's Global Stress Index (YCGSI; Findley et al. 2003)	Psychosocial stress	Psychosocial stress in children with OCD	7 to 17 years	Self and proxy assessment by questionnaire and interview with both informants with the clinician

Table 2. (Continued)

Anxiety disorder	Questionnaire	Measure	Factors	Age	Form(s)
Generalized Anxiety Disorder	Penn State Worry Questionnaire for Children (Chorpita et al., 1997)	Worries	Frequency and intensity of the worry	8 to 18 years	Self-assessment
	Worry Domains Questionnaire (WDQ) for Adolescents (Fournier, 1997; Tallis et al., 1992)	Subjects of worry	Self-confidence/Authoritarianism Performance/Consequences Finances Security/boundaries Adverse consequences	Adolescents	Self-assessment
State of Posttraumatic Stress	Child Post-Traumatic Stress Reaction Index (CPTS-RI; Frederick et al., 1992)	Posttraumatic reactions	Severity of posttraumatic reactions	6 to 18 years	Self-assessment or semi-structured interview
Phobias	The Fear Survey Schedule for Children–Revised (FSSC-R; Ollendick,1983)	Specific fears	Fear of Failure and Criticism Fear of the Unknown Fear of Injury and Small Animals Fear of Danger and Death Medical Fears	7 to 18 years	Self-assessment Proxy assessment

CONCLUSION

It was not our ambition in this chapter to present an exhaustive overview of the current state of the psychiatric nosology of anxiety disorders in children and adolescents, nor of the full range of scales and questionnaires relating to these disorders.

We have, however, attempted here to offer an up-to-date account of the place of categorical and dimensional approaches to nosology, which are increasingly perceived as complementary and indissociable in both assessment and therapy for psychopathological disorders in general and for anxiety disorders in children in particular.

Recent classifications, notably the DSM-5, have converged toward the reconciliation of the two approaches, reinforcing the direction of recent clinical research on both assessment and therapy.

It also seemed to us necessary to better specify the place, relevance and practical value of scales and instruments for assessing anxiety in children in its various clinical forms. We also highlighted the value of these instruments in the context of cognitive and behavioral therapy.

Finally, we reaffirmed the importance of multiple information sources (child, parent, other close adult) in identifying and assessing anxiety disorders in children as completely as possible in their various clinical expressions, as well as the importance of being able to use these multiple information sources to improve care—which, in the case of cognitive and behavioral therapies, includes the environment and the child's parents.

REFERENCES

Achenbach, T. M., and Rescorla, Achenbach, T. M., and Rescorla, L. A. (2000). Manual for the ASEBA preschool forms and profiles. Burlington, VT: Research Center for Children, Youth, and Families, University of Vermont.

Achenbach, T. M. (1978). The Child Behaviour profile. I. Boys aged 6-11. *Journal of Consulting and Clinical Psychology,* 46, 478-488.

Achenbach, T. M. (1991). Manual for the Child Behavior Checklist/4-18 and 1991 Profile. Burlington, VT: University of Vermont, Department of Psychiatry.

Achenbach, T. M. (1992). Manual for the child behavior checklist/2–3 and 1992 profile. Burlington: Department of Psychiatry, University of Vermont.

Achenbach, T. M., and Edelbrock, C. S. (1978). The classification of child psychopathology: A review and analysis of empirical efforts. *Psychological Bulletin*, 85(6), 1275-1301.

Achenbach, T. M., and Edelbrock, C. S. (1981). Behavioral problems and competencies reported by parents of normal and disturbed children aged four through sixteen. *Monographs of the society for research in child development,* 46(1), 1-82.

Achenbach, T. M., and Rescorla, L. A. (2001*). Manual for the ASEBA School-Age Forms and Profils.* Burlington, VT: University of Vermont, Research Center for Children Youth and Families, 238.

American Psychiatric Association. (2003). Manuel diagnostique et statistique des troubles mentaux. (4e ed.). Paris: Masson; [texte révisé].

American Psychiatric Association. (2013). Diagnostic and statistical manual of mental disorders. (5th ed.). Arlington, VA: American Psychiatric Publishing.

American Psychiatric Association. (1980). Diagnostic and Statistical Manual of mental disorders. (3rd ed.). Washington, DC: American Psychiatric Association.

Bayer, J. K., Sansan, A. V., and Hemphill, S. A. (2006). Children's moods, fears, and worries: Development of an early childhood parent questionnaire. *Journal of Emotional and Behavioral Disorders,* 14, 41-49.

Beck, A. T., Brown, G., Steer, R. A., Eidelson, J. I., and Riskind, J. H. (1987). Differentiating anxiety and depression utilizing the Cognition Checklist. *Journal of Abnormal Psychology*, 96, 179–186.

Beidel, D. C., Turner, S. M., and Morris T. L. (1995). A new inventory to asses childhood social anxiety and phobia : The Social Phobia and Anxiety Inventory for Children. *Psychological Assessment,* 7(1), 73-79.

Beidel, D. C., Turner, S. M., and Morris T. L. (2000). Social Phobia and Anxiety Inventory for Children (SPAIC): Manual. New York: Toronto, MHS, Multi-Health Systems Incorporation.

Berg, C., Rapoport, J. L., and Flament, M. (1985). The Leyton Obsessional Inventory-Child Version. *Psychopharmacology Bulletin. National Institute Of Mental Health,* 21(4), 1057-1059.

Berg, C., Whitaker, A., Davies, M., and Flament, M. F. (1988). The survey form of the Leyton Obsessional Inventory-Child Version : Norms from an epidemiological study. *Journal of the American Academy of Child and Adolescent Psychiatry,*27, 759-763.

Birmaher, B., Brent, D. A., Chiapetta, L., Bridge, J., Monga, S., and Baugher, M. (1999). Psychometric properties of the Screen for Child Anxiety Related Emotional Disorders (SCARED): a replication study. *Journal of the American Academy of Child and Adolescent Psychiatry,* 38(10), 1230-1236.

Birmaher, B., Khetarpal, S., Brent, D., Cully, M., Balach, L., Kaufman, J., et al. (1997). The Screen for Child Anxiety Related Emotional Disorders (SCARED): Scale construction and psychometric characteristics. *Journal of the American Academy of Child and Adolescent Psychiatry,* 36(4),545-553.

Bouvard, M. (Eds.). (2008). Echelles et questionnaires d'évaluation chez l'enfant et l'adolescent. Paris: Masson.

Bouvard, M., and Cottraux, J. (Eds.). (2005). Protocoles et échelles d'évaluation en psychiatrie et en psychologie. Paris: Masson.

Boyd, R. C., Ginsburg, G. S., Lambert, S. F., Cooley M. R., and Campbell K. D. M. (2003) Screen for Child Anxiety Related Emotional Disorders (SCARED): psychometric properties in an African-American parochial high school sample. *Journal of the American Academy of Child and Adolescent Psychiatry,* 42(10), 1188-1196.

Brown, T. A., and Barlow, D. H. (2009). A proposal for a dimensional classification system based on the shared features of the DSM-IV anxiety and mood disorders: implications for assesment and treatment. *Psychological Assessment,* 21(3), 256-271.

Campbell, M. A., Rapee, R. M., and Spence, S. (2001). Developmental changes in the interpretation of rating format on a questionnaire measure of worry. *Clinical Psychologist*, 5, 49–59.

Chahed M. Contributions of the Child Behavior Checklist and Youth Self-Report to the study of behavioral and emotional problems among Tunisian children adolescents [dissertation]. Nanterre, France: Université de Paris Ouest; 2010.

Chavira, D., Stein, M. B., Bailey, K., and Stein, M. T. (2004). Child anxiety in primary care : prevalent but untreated. *Depression and Anxiety,* 20(4), 155-164.

Chorpita, B. F., Tracey, S. A., Brown, T. A., Collica, T. J., and Barlow, D. H. (1997). Assessment of worry in children and adolescents: An adaptation of the Penn State Worry Questionnaire. *Behaviour Research and Therapy,* 35(6), 569-581.

Clark, D. M., Ball, S., and Pape,D. (1991). An experimental investigation of thought suppression. *Behaviour Research and Therapy,* 29, 253-257.

Clark, D. M., Winton, E., and Thynn,L. (1993). A further experimental investigation of thought suppression. *Behaviour Research and Therapy,* 31, 207-210.

Costello, E. J., Egger, H. L., and Angold, A. (2005). The developmental epidemiology of anxiety disorders : Phenomenology, prevalence and comorbidity. *Child and Adolescent Psychiatric Clinics of North America*, 14(4), 631-648.

Costello, E. J., Mustillo, S., Erkanli, A., Keeler, G., and Angold, A. (2003). Prevalence and development of psychiatric disorders in childhood and adolescence. *Archives of General Psychiatry,* 60(8), 837-844.

Crocetti, E., Hale, W. W. III., Fermani, A., Raaijmakers, Q., and Meeus, W. (2009). Psychometric properties of the Screen for Child Anxiety Related Emotional Disorders (SCARED) in the general italian adolescent population: A validation and a comparison between Italy and the Netherlands. *Journal of Anxiety Disorders,* 23(6), 824-829.

Diler, R. S., Birmaher, B., Brent, D. A., Axelson, D. A., Firinciogulari, S., Chiapetta, B. S., et al. (2004). Phenomenology of panic disorder in youth. *Depression and Anxiety,* 20(1), 39-43.

Doerfler, L. A., Toscano P. F. Jr., and Connor, D. F. (2008). Separation anxiety and panic disorder in clinical referred youth. *Journal of Anxiety Disorders,* 22(4), 602-611.

Essau, C. A., Leung, P. W. L., Conradt, J., Cheng, H., and Wong, T. (2008). Anxiety symptoms in Chinese and German adolescents: their relationship with early learning experiences, perfectionism and learning motivation. *Depression and Anxiety,* 25, 801–810.

Essau, C. A., Sakano, Y., Ishikawa, S., and Sasagawa, S. (2004). Anxiety symptoms in Japanese and in German children. *Behaviour Research and Therapy,* 42, 601–612.

Essau, C. A., Conradt, J., and Petermann, F. (1999). Frequency and comorbidity of social phobia and social fears in adolescents. *Behaviour Research and Therapy,* 37(9), 831-843.

Essau, C. A., Muris, P., and Ederer, E. (2002). Reliability and validity of the Spence Children's Anxiety Scale and the Screen for Child Anxiety Related Emotional Disorders in german children. *Journal of Behaviour Therapy and Experimental Psychiatry,* 33(1), 1-18.

Findley, D. B., Leckman, J. F., Katsovich, L., Lin, H., Zhang, H., Grantz, H., et al. (2003). Development of the Yale Children's Global Stress Index

(YCGSI) and its applications in children and adolescents with Tourete's syndrome and obsessive compulsive disorder. *Journal of the American Academy of Child and Adolescent Psychiatry,* 42(4), 450-457.

Fombonne, E. (1992). Parent reports on behavior and competencies among 6-11 year old French children. *European Child and Adolescent Psychiatry,* 1, 249-259.

Fombonne, E. (1994). The Chartres study: prevalence of psychiatric disorders among French school-aged children. *British Journal of Psychiatry,* 164(1), 69-79.

Fombonne, E., Chedan, F., and Carradec, A. M. (1988). Le Child Behavior Checklist: un instrument pour la recherche en psychiatrie de l'enfant. *Psychiatrie et Psychobiologie*, 3(6), 409-418.

Fournier, S. Worry themes and tendency to worry among a teenage sample. Unpublished Maters thesis [dissertation]. Quebec, Canada: Laval University; 1997.

Frederick, C., Pynoos, R. S., and Nader, K. (1992). Childhood Post-Traumatic Stress Reaction Index (CPTS-RI). Copyrighted instrument. Available on request from Frederick and Pynoos, 760 Westwood Plaza, Los Angeles, CA 90024 or Nader, P.O. Box 2251, Laguna Hills, CA 92654.

Gladman, M., and Lancaster, S. (2003). A Review of the Behaviour Assessment System for Children. *School Psychology International,* 24(3), 276-291.

Goodman R, Ford T, H Simmons, Gatward R, and Meltzer H. (2003). Using the Strengths and Difficulties Questionnaire (SDQ) to screen for child psychiatric disorders in a community sample. *International Review of Psychiatry,* 15 (1-2),166-172.

Goodman, R. (1997). The Strengths and Difficulties Questionnaire: a research note. *Journal of Child Psychology and Psychiatry,* 38, 581–586.

Goodman, R. (2001). Psychometric Properties of the Strengths and Difficulties Questionnaire.

Goodman, R., Meltzer, H., and Bailey, V. (1998). The Strengths and Difficulties Questionnaire: a pilot study on the validity of the self-report version. *European Child and Adolescent Psychiatry,* 7,125–130.

Goodman, R., and Scott, S. (1999). Comparing the Strengths and Difficulties Questionnaire and the Child Behavior Checklist: is small beautiful? *Journal of Abnormal Child Psychology,* 27,17–24.

Goodwin, R., and Gotlib, I. H. (2004). Panic attacks and psychopathology among youth. *Acta Psychiatrica Scandinavica,* 109(3), 216-221.

Gosselin, P., Langlois, F., Freeston, M. H., Ladouceur, R., Dugas, M. J., and Pelletier, O. (2002). The cognitive Avoidance Questionnaire (CAQ): development and validation among adult and adolescent samples. *Journal of Cognitive and Behavioral Therapy,*12(1), 24-37.

Gren-Landell, M., Tillfors, M., Furmark, T., Bohlin, G., Andersson, G., and Svedin, C. G. (2009). Social phobia in swedish adolescents, prevalence and gender differences. *Social Psychiatry and Psychiatric Epidemiology,* 44(1), 1-7.

Hale, W. W. III, Crocetti, E, Raaijmakers, Q., and Meeus W. (2011). A meta-analysis of the cross-cultural psychometric properties of the Screen for Child Anxiety Related Emotional Disorders (SCARED). *The Journal of Child Psychology and Psychiatry,* 51(1), 80-90.

Hale, W. W. III, Raaijmakers, Q., Muris, P., and Meeus, W. (2005). Psychometric properties of the Screen for Child Anxiety Related Emotional Disorders (SCARED) in the general adolescent population. *Journal of the American Academy of Child and Adolescent Psychiatry,* 44(3), 283-290.

Hale, W. W. III, Raaijmakers, Q., Muris, P., Van Hoof, A., and Meeus, W. (2008). Developmental trajectories of adolescent anxiety disorder symptoms: a 5-year prospective community study. *Journal of the American Academy of Child and Adolescent Psychiatry,* 47(5), 556-564.

Hudziak, J. J., Achenbach, T. M., Althoff, R. R, and Pine, D. S. (2007). A dimensional approach to developmental psychopathology. *International Journal of Methods in Psychiatric Research,* 16(1), 16-23.

Ishikawa, S., Sato, H., and Sasagawa, S. (2009). Anxiety disorder symptoms in Japanese children and adolescents. *Journal of Anxiety Disorders,* 23, 104–111.

Kaslow, N. J., Stark, K. D., Printz, B., Livingston, R., and Tsai, S. L. (1992). Cognitive triad inventory for children: Development and relation to depression and anxiety. *Journal of Clinical Child Psychology*, 21, 339–347.

Keeton, C. P., Kolos, A. C., and Walkup, J. T. (2009). Pediatric generalized anxiety disorder. *Pediatric Drugs,* 11(3), 171-183.

Klasen H., Woerner W., Wolke D. et al. (2000), Comparing the German versions of the Strengths and Difficulties Questionnaire (SDQ-Deu) and the Child Behavior Checklist. *European Child and Adolescent Psychiatry,* 9, 271–276.

Klein, R. G. (1994). Anxiety disorders. In M. Rutter, E. Taylor, and L. Hersov (Eds), Child and Adolescent Psychiatry: Modern approaches (pp. 351-374). Oxford: Blackwell Scientific Publications.

Klein, R. G. (2009). Anxiety disorders. *The Journal of Child Psychology and Psychiatry,* 50(1-2), 153-162.

Koskelainen M., Sourander A., and Kaljonen A. (2000), The Strengths and Difficulties Questionnaire among Finnish school-aged children and adolescents. *European Child and Adolescent Psychiatry,* 9, 277–284.

Krueger, R., and Piasecki, T. (2002). Toward a dimensional and psychometrically-informed approach to conceptualizing psychopathology. *Behaviour Research and Therapy*, 40(5), 485-499.

La Greca, A. M., and López, N. (1998). Social anxiety among adolescents: linkage with peer relations and friendships. *Journal of Abnormal Child Psychology,* 26, 83–94.

La Greca, A. M., and Stone, W. L. (1993). Social Anxiety Scale for Children-Revised: factor structure and concurrent validity. *Journal of clinical Child psychology,* 22, 17-27.

Lavy, E. H., and van den Hout, M. A. (1990). Thought suppression induces intrusions. *Behavioural Psychotherapy,* 18, 251-258.

Layne, A. E., Bernat, H. D., Victor, A. M., and Bernstein, G. A. (2009). Generalized anxiety disorder in a nonclinical sample of children : symptom presentation and predictors of impairment. *Journal of Anxiety Disorders,* 23(2), 283-289.

Lewinsohn, P. M., Gotlib, I. H., Lewinsohn, M., Seeley, J. R., and Allen, N. B. (1998). Gender differences in anxiety disorders and anxiety symptoms in adolescents. *Journal of Abnormal Psychology,* 107(1), 109-117.

March, J. S., Parker, J. D. A., Sullivan, K., Stallings, P., and Conners, C. K. (1997). The multidimensional anxiety scale for children (MASC): Factor structure, reliability and validity. *Journal of the American Academy of Child and Adolescent Psychiatry*, 36, 554–565.

March, J. S. (1997). Manual for the Multidimensional Anxiety Scale for Children (MASC). Toronto : Multi-Health Systems Incorporation.

Mellon, R. C., and Moutavelis, A. G. (2007). Structure, developmental course, and correlates of children's anxiety disorder-related behaviour in a Hellenic community sample. *Journal of Anxiety Disorders,* 21, 1–21.

Monga, S., Birmaher, B., Chiapetta, L., Brent, D., Kaufman, J., Bridge, J., et al. (2000). Screen for Child Related Emotional Disorders (SCARED): Convergent and divergent validity. *Depression and Anxiety,* 12(2), 85-91.

Muris, P., and Broeren, S. (2009). Twenty-five years of research on childhood anxiety disorders : publication trend between 1982 and 2006 and a selective review of literature. *Journal of Child and Family Studies,* 18(4), 388-395.

Muris, P., Merckelbach, H., Ollendick, T., King, N., K., and Bogie, N. (2002). Three traditional and three new childhood anxiety questionnaires: their reliability and validity in a normal adolescent sample. *Behaviour Research and Therapy,* 40(7), 753-772.

Muris, P., Schmidt, H., and Merckelbach, H. (2000). Correlations among two self-report questionnaires for measuring DSM-defined anxiety disorder symptoms in children: the screen for child anxiety related emotional disorders and the Spence Children's Anxiety Scale. *Personality and Individual Differences,* 28, 333–346.

Muris, P., Schmidt, H., Engelbrecht, P., and Perold, M. (2002). DSM-IV-defined anxiety disorder symptoms in South African children. *Journal of the American Academy of Child and Adolescent Psychiatry,* 41, 1360–1368.

Nauta, M., Scholing, A., Rapee, R., Abott, M., Spence, S. H., and Waters, A. (2004). A parent-report measure of children's anxiety: psychometric properties and comparison with child-report in a clinic and normal sample. *Behaviour Research and Therapy*, 42(7), 813-839.

Ollendick, T. H. (1983). Reliability and validity of the Revised Fear Survey Schedule for Children (FSSC-R). *Behavior Research and Therapy*, 21, 685–692.

Organisation Mondiale de la Santé (OMS). CIM-10 / ICD-10 Classification internationale des troubles mentaux et des troubles du comportement : critères diagnostiques pour la recherche. Paris : Masson, 2000.

Ranta, K., Kaltiala-Heino, R., Rantanen, P., and Marttunen, M. (2009). Social phobia in finnish general adolescent population : prevalence, comorbidity, individual and family correlates, and service use. *Depression and Anxiety,* 26(6), 528-536.

Rao, P. A., Beidel, D. C., Turner S. M., Ammerman, R. T., Crosby, L. E., and Fallee, F. R. (2007). Social anxiety disorder in childhood and adolescence: descriptive psychopathology. *Behaviour Research and Therapy,* 45(6), 1181-1197.

Research on Pediatric Psychopharmacology Anxiety Study Group. (2002). The Pediatric Anxiety Rating Scale (PARS): development and psychometric properties. *Journal of the American Academy of Child and Adolescent Psychiatry,* 41, 1061-1069.

Reynolds, C. R., and Richmond, B. O. (1985). Manual for the Revised Children's Manifest Anxiety Scale. Los Angeles: Western Psychological Association.

Rusinek, S. and Hautekeete, M. (1999). Instrument d'étude des schemas des enfants: L'inventaire des schemas précoces pour enfants (ISPE). *Journal of Behavioral and Cognitive Therapy,* 9(2), 55-61.

Schmidt, N., Joiner Jr., T, Young, J., and Telch, M. (1995). Schema questionnaire : Investigation of psychometric properties and hierarchical structure of a mesure of maladaptative schemas. *Cognitive Therapy and Research,* 19(3), 295-321.

Schniering, C. A., and Lyneham, H. J. (2007). The Children's Automatic Thoughts Scale in a clinical sample: Psychometric properties and clinical utility. *Behaviour Research and Therapy,* 45, 1931–1940.

Schniering, C. A., and Rapee, R. M. (2002). Development and validation of a measure of children's automatic thoughts: The Children's Automatic Thoughts Scale. *Behaviour Research and Therapy,* 40, 1091–1109.

Schniering, C. A., and Rapee, R. M. (2004a). The relationship between automatic thoughts and negative emotions in children and adolescents: A test of the cognitive content-specificity hypothesis. *Journal of Abnormal Psychology,* 113, 464–470.

Schniering, C. A., and Rapee, R. M. (2004b). The structure of negative self-statements among children and adolescents: A confirmatory factor-analytic approach. *Journal of Abnormal Child Psychology,* 32(1), 95-109.

Schniering, C. A., Hudson, J. L., and Rapee, R. M. (2000). Issues in the diagnosis and assessment of anxiety disorders in children and adolescents. *Clinical Psychology Review*, 20, 453–478.

Spence, S. H. (1998). A measure of anxiety symptoms among children. *Behaviour Research and Therapy,* 36(5), 545-566.

Spence, S. H., Rapee, R., McDonald, C., and Ingram, M. (2001). The structure of anxiety symptoms among preschoolers. *Behaviour Research and Therapy,* 39, 1293–1316.

Spence, S. H. (1997). The structure of anxiety symptoms among children: a confirmatory factor analytic study. *Journal of Abnormal Psychology and Psychiatry,* 106(2), 280-297.

Spielberger, C. (1973). Manual for the State-Trait Anxiety Inventory for children. Palo Alto, CA: Consulting Psychologists Press.

Stark, K. D., Best, L. R., and Adam, T. (1990). Development and psychometric evaluation of a depressogenic thoughts questionnaire for children, Unpublished manuscript. In, Schniering, C. A. and Rapee, R. M.

(2002). Development and validation of a measure of children's automatic thoughts: the children's automatic thoughts scale. *Behaviour Research and Therapy,* 40, 1091–1109.

Storch, E.A., Murphy, T. K., Adkins, J. W., Lewin, A. B., Geffken, G. R., Johns, N. B., et al. (2006). The Children's Yale Brown Obsessive Compulsive Sclae : psychometric properties of child-and parent-report formats. *Journal of Anxiety Disorders,* 20, 1055-1070.

Su, L., Wang, K., Fan, F., Su, Y., and Gao, X. (2008). Reliability and validity of the Screen for Child Anxiety Related Emotional Disorders (SCARED) in Chinese children, *Journal of Anxiety Disorders,* 22(4), 612-621.

Tallis, F., Eysenck, M., and Mathews, A. (1992). A questionnaire for the measurement of nonpathological worry. *Personality and Individual Differences,* 13, 161-168.

Tortella-Feliu, M., Balle, M., Servera, M., and de la Banda, G. (2005). Psychometric properties of the Catalan version of the Spence Children's Anxiety Scale (SCAS). *Psicologia Conductual-Revista Internacional de Psicologia Clinica y de la Salud,* 13, 111–123.

Van Oort, F. V. A., Greaves-Lord, K., Verhulst, F. C., Ormel, J., and Huizink, A. C. (2009). The developmental course of anxiety symptoms during adolescence: the TRAILS study. *The Journal of Child Psychology and Psychiatry,* 50(10), 1209-1217.

Van-Roy, B., Kristensen, H., Groholt, B., and Clench-Aas, J. (2009). Prevalence and characteristics of significant social anxiety in children aged 8-13 years. *Social Psychiatry and Psychiatric Epidemiology,* 44(5), 407-415.

Vera, L. (Eds.). (2009). *TCC chez l'enfant et l'adolescent.* Paris: Masson.

Vera, L.(1996). Echelle Comportementale d'Anxiété Phobique (ECAP): Construction, validation et intérêt en clinique enfant-adolescent. *Neuropsychiatrie de l'enfance et de l'adolescence,* 44 (9-10), 429-438.

Verhulst, F. C., and Van der Ende, J. (1992). Agreement between parents' reports and adolescents' self-reports of problem behavior. *The Journal of Child Psychology and Psychiatry,* 33(6), 1011-1023.

Vigil-Colet, A., Canals, J., Cosi, S., Lorenzo-Seva, U., Ferrando, P. J., Hernández-Martínez, C., et al. (2009). The factorial structure of the 41-item version of the Screen for Child Anxiety Related Emotional Disorders (SCARED) in a spanish population of 8 to 12 years-old, *International Journal of Clinical and Health Psychology,* 9(2), 313-327.

Wells, A., Stopa, L., and Clark, D. M. (1993). The social cognitions questionnaire. Not published manuscript. University of Oxford.

Whiteside, S. P., and Brown, A. M. (2008). Exploring the utility of the Spence Children's Anxiety Scales parent- and child-report forms in a North American sample. *Journal of Anxiety Disorders,* 22, 1440–1446.

Whiteside, S., Gryczkowski, M., Ale, C., Brown-Jacobson, A., McCarthy, D. (2013). Development of Child- and Parent-Report Measures of Behavioral Avoidance Related to Childhood Anxiety Disorders. *Behavior Therapy,* 44, 325-337.

Wren, F. J., Berg, E. A., Heiden, L. A., Kynnamon, C. J., Ohlson, L. A., Bridge, et al. (2007). Childhood anxiety in a diverse primary care population: parent-child reports, ethnicity and SCARED factor structure. *Journal of the American Academy of Child and Adolescent Psychiatry,* 46(3), 332-340.

Wren, F. J., Bridge, J. A., and Birmaher, B. (2004). Screening for childhood anxiety symptoms in primary care : integrating child and parent reports. *Journal of the American Academy of Child and Adolescent Psychiatry,* 43(11), 1364-1371.

Young, J. 1990. Cognitive Therapy for Personality Disorders: A schema-Focused Approach. Professional Resource Exchange, Sarasota.

Young, J. Early Maladaptative Schemas. Unpublished manuscript, 1991. Cité dans: Rusinek, S. and Hautekeete,M. (1999). Instrument d'étude des schemas des enfants :L'inventaire des schemas précoces pour enfants (ISPE). *Journal of Behavioral and Cognitive Therapy,* 9(2), 55-61.

Young, J., and Klosko, J. (Eds.). (1993). *Je réinvente ma vie.* Editions de l'Homme: Montréal.

Zebdi, R. Contribution of the SCARED (Screen for Child Anxiety Related Emotional Disorders), CBCL (Child Behavior Checklist) and Kiddie-SADS (Schedule for Affective Disorders and Schizophrenia for School-Age Children-) to the assessment of anxiety disorders among school-age children. [dissertation]. Nanterre, France: Université de Paris Ouest; 2011.

Zebdi, R., and Petot, D. (2013). Contribution de la Screen for Child Anxiety Related Emotional Disorders au dépistage et au diagnostic des troubles anxieux chez l'enfant d'âge scolaire. *L'Evolution Psychiatrique,* http:// dx.doi.org/10.1016/j.evopsy.2013.05.002.

In: Anxiety Disorders
Editor: Shiloh Angelus Roman
ISBN: 978-1-63117-392-9

Chapter 3

GENETICS OF ANXIETY DISORDERS

Alessandra Minelli [*] ***and Elisabetta Maffioletti***
Department of Molecular and Translational Medicine,
University of Brescia, Brescia, Italy

ABSTRACT

There is considerable evidence that genetic determinants could play a role in the pathogenesis of anxiety disorders. Linkage studies, association studies and genome-wide association studies (GWASs) have identified genetic profiles associated with anxiety disorders such as panic disorder (PD), post-traumatic stress disorder (PTSD), obsessive compulsive disorder (OCD), generalized anxiety disorder (GAD) and social anxiety disorder (SAD). There is not one specific gene that causes anxiety, but combinations of genes seem to be at play. Furthermore, environmental factors, like stressful life events, may trigger an anxiety disorder more easily in people who have a genetic predisposition to the illness. However, the mechanisms are far from a complete understanding.

To date, the most studied genetic variant is the serotonin transporter polymorphism (5-HTTLPR), which has been indicated as a risk factor for anxiety disorders, also affecting relative treatments. Other studies regarding the genetic susceptibility to anxiety disorders have focused on studying variants in neurotrophic genes (e.g., BDNF) and in the

[*] Corresponding author: Alessandra Minelli - Department of Molecular and Translational Medicine, Biology and Genetic Division, University of Brescia, Viale Europa, 11 - 25123 Brescia, Italy. Tel.: +39 030 3501596; Fax: +39 030 3533513 E-mail address: alessandra.minelli@med.unibs.it.

hypothalamic-pituitary-adrenal axis (HPA) related genes (e.g., FKBP5, CRHR1, NR3C1). In particular, candidate gene approach studies have investigated variants in genes related to HPA and corticotropin-releasing hormone (CRH) pathways because of their central role in the adaptation of the organism to stress.

Finally, investigations of susceptibility genes for anxiety disorders can be helped from the study of the genetic factors underlying personality traits, such as neuroticism and harm avoidance, that constitute risk factors for anxiety disorders.

The identification of genetic variants involved in anxiety may have implications for the optimization of therapeutic interventions because they have been largely shown to represent predictors of poorer response.

INTRODUCTION

Anxiety is a basic human emotion that everyone experiences at times. Many people feel anxious, or nervous, when faced with a problem at work, before taking a test, or making an important decision. Anxiety is not typically pathologic, but commonly adaptive when it facilitates avoidance of danger. Anxiety disorders, however, are different. They can cause such distress that it interferes with a person's ability to lead a normal life. For people with anxiety disorders, worry and fear are constant and overwhelming.

Diagnostic criteria for anxiety disorders are described in the Diagnostic and Statistical Manual of Mental Disorders (DSM, current version IV-TR, American Psychiatric Association) and in the International Classification of Diseases (ICD, current version 10, World Health Organization). The most important are the following: panic disorder (PD), post-traumatic stress disorder (PTSD), obsessive-compulsive disorder (OCD), generalized anxiety disorder (GAD), social anxiety disorder (SAD) and specific phobias.

Many anxiety disorders share common clinical features such as extensive anxiety, physiologic anxiety symptoms, behavioral disturbances such as extreme avoidance of feared objects, and associated distress or impairment (Craske et al., 2009; Shear et al., 2007). However, narrowly categorized anxiety disorders such as panic disorder, agoraphobia, social phobia, and subtypes of specific phobias also exhibit a substantial degree of phenotypical diversity and heterogeneity (Craske et al., 2009; LeBeau et al., 2010; Shear et al., 2007).

Furthermore, anxiety disorders often co-occur in the same individual, either simultaneously or sequentially, with other psychiatric disorders such as major depressive disorder (MDD) and alcohol use disorders (AUD). In particular, anxiety disorders and MDD share a long, close history in psychiatric nosology and treatment, and high rates of comorbidity between anxiety and depression (approximately 40-50%) are well established (Fava et al., 2000; Maser and Cloninger, 1990). This issue raises questions since it is largely demonstrated that remission is significantly less likely or takes longer to occur in MDD patients with anxiety disorders in comorbidity compared to those with non-anxious depression. Furthermore, the side effect frequency, intensity and burden, as well as the number of serious adverse events, are all greater in anxious depressed patients (Fava et al., 2008; Maser and Cloninger, 1990).

Thus, for dealing with the issue of the biological bases of anxiety disorders, it is necessary to take into account all these aspects, wondering if there could be common mechanisms shared between different anxiety disorders or specific mechanisms for each specific anxiety disorder. Again, it is important to consider if the data to date available are affected by possible comorbidities present in the sample studied and, finally, whether the use of endophenotypes, such as personality traits, can be a useful tool for identifying susceptibility genes for anxiety disorders.

BIOLOGICAL BASES OF ANXIETY AND ANXIETY DISORDERS

The biological bases of anxiety and anxiety disorders concern alterations in the mechanisms which mediate stress response, in particular the corticotropin-releasing hormone (CRH) network and the hypothalamic-pituitary-adrenal (HPA) axis. CRH is a peptide which plays a key role in neuroendocrine, autonomic and behavioral adaptation to stress. Under stressful conditions, CRH neurons in the hypothalamus stimulate the activation of HPA. Stressful changes in the internal or external environment are conveyed to the central nervous system (CNS) and integrated in the hypothalamus. CRH activates adrenocorticotropin (ACTH) secretion from the anterior pituitary gland, which in turn stimulates glucocorticoid release from the adrenal cortex. The CRH effect at this level is amplified by arginine vasopressin (AVP), which is secreted by hypothalamic CRH neurons (Bonfiglio et al., 2011). Glucocorticoids (cortisol in humans and cortisone in rodents) produce a stress response through their actions on multiple target organs, but they are also critical for terminating it, via a negative feedback at different levels of the HPA. A prolonged or excessive activation of this system has been implicated in the pathogenesis of anxiety disorders, also involving an impaired sensitivity of glucocorticoid receptors (GRs) (Binder, 2009). Another way by which CRH may play a role in the pathophysiology of anxiety is the regulation of brainstem neuromodulatory systems, such as serotonergic systems. CRH acts in the dorsal raphe nucleus, the major source for serotonin (5-HT) in the brain, altering the activity of specific subsets of serotonergic neurons and influencing stress-related behavior (Fox and Lowry, 2013). The role of several other neurotransmitter systems in the mediation of different anxious symptoms has been reported in literature. The excitatory amino acid transmitter glutamate has been suggested to play a pivotal role in the pathogenesis of anxiety disorders by mediating limbic neurotransmission. Interestingly, acute stress has been shown to enhance glutamate release in the amygdala; moreover, glutamatergic NMDA receptors can control CRH release and exert a significant influence on the activity of monoaminergic pathways (Riaza Bermudo-Soriano et al., 2012). The amygdala is a brain area basically characterized by low neuronal firing, due to a strong inhibitory tone maintained by γ-aminobutyric acid (GABA)-ergic neurons; when a signal indicates threat, defensive circuits are activated. Conversely, signals which don't predict danger are suppressed. In pathological states, this inhibition can become impaired and neutral signals can cause non-adaptive fear and anxiety. Therefore, alterations in GABAergic transmission are strongly implicated in anxiety disorders, as proven also by the fact that benzodiazepines exert their anxiolytic effects through the allosteric modulation of GABA receptors, thus enhancing inhibitory activity (Mohler, 2012). Besides the above-mentioned neurotransmitter systems, also dopaminergic, noradrenergic, cannabinergic and neuropeptidergic (e.g., neuropeptide Y, neuropeptide S, cholecystokinin) systems have been also shown to be involved in the neurochemistry of anxiety (Faludi et al., 2012). Finally, another important, but often disregarded system potentially involved in anxiety mechanisms is the polyamine system. Owing to their interactions with several transmembrane channels, polyamines can influence the electrical properties of excitable cells, such as neurons. Additionally, they can influence the properties of several neurotransmitter pathways. Interestingly, an increase in polyamine levels has been observed as a part of behavioral response to stress (Fiori and Turecki, 2008).

Molecular Genetic Methods

Molecular genetic search strategies used for the investigation of the biological mechanisms of complex disorders are based on different, but often complementary methods.

Linkage studies involve genotyping anonymous DNA markers across the genome in large pedigrees or affected relative pairs to determine the approximate chromosomal location of susceptibility genes. Genetic linkage analysis is a powerful tool to detect the chromosomal location of disease genes and it is based on the observation that genes that reside physically close on a chromosome remain linked during meiosis. For several diseases for which the underlying genetic defect is not known, the identification of the chromosomal location of the disease gene is the first step in its eventual isolation. Thus, this approach can be useful since it does not require *a priori* prediction of the gene locus; however, it has relatively low power to detect genes of small effect, that is the most frequent condition for susceptibility genes of complex and multi-factorial diseases as anxiety disorders.

In contrast to linkage studies, genetic association studies involve genotyping candidate genes based on a hypothesized involvement in disease pathogenesis. Genetic association studies test for a correlation between a disease status and genetic variation to identify candidate genes or genomic regions that contribute to a specific disease. A significantly higher frequency of a single-nucleotide polymorphism (SNP) allele or genotype in a series of individuals affected with a disease, compared to healthy controls, can be interpreted as meaning that the tested variant increases the risk for that specific disease. Indeed, a significant genetic association may be interpreted as a direct association, in which the genotyped SNP is the true causal variant conferring disease susceptibility, or an indirect association, in which the genotyped SNP is in linkage disequilibrium (LD) with the true causal variant. However, association studies may also produce spurious results because of undetected differences in the population substructure unrelated to the disease. For this reason, all the significant associations require a confirmation in other samples (replication samples) and may require resequencing of the candidate region, dense genotyping of all the available SNPs, or functional studies to confirm the role of a putative mutation. Moreover, in addition to the selection of candidate genes, in association studies it is equally important to choose appropriate SNPs within a given gene. Apparently contradictory results for a given gene may often be explained by the investigators' testing of different polymorphisms, which may give rise to discrepant results depending on their true proximity (LD) to the actual genetic site, causing the illness within a given gene. A possible alternative to SNP investigations is the determination of haplotypes, consisting of a number of linked markers within a single gene. Finally, even if SNPs are the most widely tested markers in association studies, microsatellite markers, insertion/deletions (ins/del), variable-number tandem repeats (VNTRs), and copy-number variations (CNVs) are also used.

A further method without *a priori* hypothesis, but technologically more recent than linkage studies, is represented by genome-wide association studies (GWASs). GWASs are a relatively new way for scientists to identify genes involved in human diseases, which has permitted an enormous progress in mapping complex traits in the last years. GWASs involve correlating allele frequencies at each of several hundreds of thousands of markers spaced throughout the genome with trait variation in a population-based sample. A GWAS is based on the premise that a causal variant is located on a haplotype, and therefore a marker allele in LD with the causal variant should show (by proxy) an association with a trait of interest. One of the advantages of the GWAS approach is that it is unbiased with respect to genomic structure and previous knowledge of the trait etiology, in contrast to candidate gene studies, where knowledge of the trait is used to identify candidate loci contributing to the trait of interest. Therefore, GWAS results hold the promise to reveal causal genes not previously suspected in disease etiology, genetic effects of non-genic DNA regions, relatively complete additive and non-additive effects and pleiotropy in an unbiased way. Since GWASs examine SNPs across the genome, they have represented a promising way to study complex, common diseases in which many genetic variations contribute to a person's risk. Indeed, these studies have clearly demonstrated that for many common disorders the predominant pattern is that of many loci, individually with small effects on phenotype. For some traits, loci of large effect have been identified. For almost all the complex traits studied in humans, the sum of the identified genetic effects comprises only a portion, generally less than half, of the estimated trait heritability. A variety of hypotheses have been proposed to explain why this might be the case, including untested rare variants, and gene–gene and gene–environment interactions.

Genetic Studies on Anxiety Disorders

The most studied anxiety disorder in association to gene variants is PD. Linkage studies have shown several potential risk loci for PD (chromosomes

1p, 4q, 7p, 11p, 15q and 20p) (Crowe et al., 2001; Fyer et al., 2006; Gelernter et al., 2001; Hamilton et al., 2003; Kaabi et al., 2006; Knowles et al., 1998; Thorgeirsson et al., 2003).

Candidate gene studies have reported association with genetic variants in the adenosine A2A receptor (ADORA2A) (Hamilton et al., 2004; Hohoff et al., 2010), the cholecystokinin B receptor (CCK-B) (Hosing et al., 2004; Miyasaka et al., 2004), the monoamine oxidase A (MAO-A) (Domschke et al., 2012; Reif et al., 2013; Reif et al., 2012; Samochowiec et al., 2004), the catechol-O-methyltransferase (COMT) (Domschke et al., 2007; Domschke et al., 2004; Karacetin et al., 2012), the serotonin 1A receptor (5-HT1A) (Blaya et al., 2010; Choe et al., 2013; Inada et al., 2003) and the glutamate decarboxylase 1 (GAD1) genes (Weber et al., 2012). To date, the published GWASs have indicated new potential candidate genes for PD, such as the transmembrane protein 132D (TMEM132D) (Erhardt et al., 2011) later confirmed by an association study (Erhardt et al., 2012), the amiloride-sensitive cation channel 1 (ACCN1) (Gregersen et al., 2012) and the bradykinin receptor B2 (BDKRB2) (Otowa et al., 2012). However, despite several studies performed and several association reported, sure specific loci have not been established and many studies have failed to replicate significant associations. Although no robust genetic finding has emerged so far, it is conceivable that panic disorder susceptibility genes will be identified in the coming years via the application of modern molecular genetic methods and through multicentric collaborations to bring together combined, large datasets.

Another widely investigated disorder is PTSD. In particular, most evidence has been provided for the insertion/deletion variants in 5-HTTLPR, the promoter region of SLC6A4 (coding for the serotonin transporter, SERT) (Gressier et al., 2013), as well as for variants in genes involved in the HPA axis, such as FK506 binding protein 5 (FKBP5) (Klengel et al., 2013; Mehta et al., 2011; Sarapas et al., 2011), and CRH receptor 1 gene (CRHR1) (Amstadter et al., 2011; White et al., 2013). A dysregulation of dopaminergic neurotransmission has also been implicated in the pathophysiology of PTSD. Several candidate gene studies have been conducted on polymorphisms in the dopamine transporter (SLC6A3, also known as DAT or DAT1), in the dopamine receptor D2 (DRD2) and in dopamine beta-hydroxylase (DBH) genes, with contrasting results (Almli et al., 2013; Digangi et al., 2013). Other associations have been reported for polymorphisms in COMT, brain derived neurotrophic factor (BDNF), regulator of G-protein signalling 2 (RGS2) and in $GABA_A$ receptor subunit alpha 2 (GABRA2) genes (Almli et al., 2013; Digangi et al., 2013; Domschke and Deckert, 2012).

The first GWAS on PTSD has been recently published, and a significant association with a variant in the retinoid-related orphan receptor alpha (RORA) gene was found (Logue et al., 2013). To date, replication results are still few and contrasting; however, several replication studies for better understanding the role of this gene are ongoing (Logue et al., 2013).

For PTSD, although few conclusive results regarding risk genes are available, a clear evidence emerges, suggesting the involvement of the serotonergic and glucocorticoid systems.

The best result arising from candidate gene studies conducted on OCD (Murphy et al., 2013b) concerns 5-HTTLPR. In particular, OCD has been associated to the long (L) allele (Bengel et al., 1999; Murphy et al., 2013b). However, some non-replications were later reported; this could be attributed to the existence of another variant, later described to convert the L allele into the equivalent of the short (S) one (Hu et al., 2006), with important consequences for the association of the L allele with the disease. An association has been found also for a haplotype including this and two other neighboring variants (Wendland et al., 2008); overall, these findings suggest an increased SERT function in OCD. Other studies found associations with variants in SLC1A1 gene (encoding the neuronal glutamate transporter EAAC1 and EAAT3) (Arnold et al., 2006; Dickel et al., 2006; Shugart et al., 2009; Stewart et al., 2007; Wang et al., 2010).

Finally, the first GWAS on OCD has revealed significant associations for SNPs in the DLGAP1 gene, expressed in the neuronal postsynaptic density complex (Stewart et al., 2013).

For other anxiety disorders, such as GAD and SAD, few associations have been shown, and positive results involve genes already indicated for the above-mentioned disorders, such as 5-HTTLPR, FKPB5 and SLC6A3 (Almli et al., 2013; Domschke and Deckert, 2012; Minelli et a!., 2013).

Genetic Studies on Anxiety-related Traits

Although the majority of genetic studies on anxiety disorders continue to define groups based on DSM-IV criteria, investigators are increasingly looking at alternatives that may more closely map on to actual genetic determinants. Many researchers have begun to focus more and more on the study of endophenotypes associated with different psychiatric disorders, in order to more fully characterize the complex pathway from genotype to phenotype (Kendler et al., 1993).

Endophenotypes in psychiatry have been defined as internal phenotypes measurable by a neurophysiological, biochemical, endocrinological, neuroanatomical, neuroimaging, cognitive, and neuropsychological technique that are heritable, cosegregate with a psychiatric illness, and yet are present before the disease is manifested (so they are not dependent on the state of the illness and can be found in non-affected family members at a higher rate than in the general population) (Gottesman and Gould, 2003). Thus, the use of endophenotypes represents a good strategy for enhancing the power of genetic studies since, as just indicated, these putative endophenotypes or intermediate phenotypes are familial or heritable traits that are thought to underlie the clinically diagnosed disorder. Furthermore, the use of endophenotypes provides added statistical power in analyses because they are typically used as quantitative phenotypes, in contrast to the DSM-IV qualitative phenotypes. The hope is that genes that may have only modest effects on the disorder would have larger effects on these more elemental traits. Personality traits are individual characteristics that influence cognition, emotions, and behavior, leading to adaptive or maladaptive responses. They are supposed to identify stable dimensional characteristics that can be quantitatively assessed in the general population and in patients affected by mental disorders (Cloninger et al., 1993). Therefore, personality traits may represent a useful endophenotype for identifying biological correlations for mental illnesses as well as common vulnerability factors.

It is well established that certain personality traits, or anxious temperament, strongly correlate with more constitutional forms of anxiety and anxiety disorders. Consequently, these psychological constructs related to anxiety have frequently been used as dimensional variables or premorbid traits for anxiety psychopathology, particularly with respect to their genetic bases and possibly specific neuronal activation patterns (Brandes and Bienvenu, 2006). These dimensions are highly heritable and stable throughout life, are correlated with emotional reactions and habits (Heath et al., 1994) and, according to the literature, approximately 30–60% of the variance in personality traits is due to genetic factors (Bouchard and Loehlin, 2001). To date, most investigators wishing to examine anxiety-related traits have focused on neuroticism (tendency toward negative emotional states) and harm avoidance (anxiety proneness). These constructs are highly correlated (Zuckerman and Cloninger, 1996); however, there is evidence that they may not be equivalent, because they are elicited using different instruments and are based on different theoretic models of personality (De Fruyt et al., 2006; Zuckerman and Cloninger, 1996).

The first study on these construct was the pioneering work by Lesch and colleagues (Lesch et al., 1996), in which a significant association between the 5-HTTLPR polymorphism and anxiety-related personality traits was demonstrated. In particular, the authors found that the presence of the 5-HTTLPR S allele was associated with higher mean neuroticism scores. Since then, 5-HTTLPR has become one of the most extensively investigated polymorphisms in studies on personality traits and generally in psychiatric disorders. A large number of studies have sought evidence of an association between 5-HTTLPR and anxiety-related personality traits. However, despite these results, the strength and nature of any association is still uncertain. Several reasons can be lead to these controversial results: 1) contrasting results were obtained using harm avoidance or neuroticism; 2) another relevant bias could be the inclusion of data from presumably healthy subjects, without any psychological screening to exclude any DSM-IV axis I psychiatric disorder; 3) ethnic differences may be a further confounding factor in several studies and meta-analyses, because the S allele is much more prevalent in Asians than in Caucasians; 4) finally, it has been critically discussed that the analysis of 5-HTTLPR is incomplete, because other polymorphisms have been found in the proximity of the ins/del locus, such as rs25531, rs25532, rs2020933 and a 17-bp variable tandem repeat in the second intron (Minelli et al., 2011a; Murphy et al., 2013a).

Candidate gene studies have reported associations with markers within other several genes, such as BDNF, cannabinoid receptor 1 (CNR1) and DRD4 (Hunnerkopf et al., 2007; Juhasz et al., 2009; Minelli et al., 2009; Szekely et al., 2004; Zhou et al., 2008), but replications generally failed (Cotton et al., 2009; Minelli et al., 2011b; Paterson et al., 1999). To date, the genes associated with anxiety-related personality traits for which several candidate studies are in agreement are tryptophan hydroxylase 1 (TPH1), which variants participate in the regulation of serotonin levels (Andre et al., 2013; Nash et al., 2005), and FKBP5, which represents a crucial regulator of GRs (Minelli et al., 2013; Shibuya et al., 2010).

Several studies provided also evidence of suggestive linkage between neuroticism/harm avoidance and several chromosomal regions (Cloninger et al., 1998; Fullerton et al., 2003; Gillespie et al., 2008; Kuo et al., 2007; Nash et al., 2004; Neale et al., 2005; Wray et al., 2008). Of the linked regions, 1q, 8p, 11q, 12q and 18q were replicated for neuroticism in various studies (Cloninger et al., 1998; Fullerton et al., 2003; Kuo et al., 2007; Neale et al., 2005). A recent study (Amin et al., 2012) has found suggestive evidence of linkage for neuroticism to 19q, 21q and 22q. Haplotype construction and analysis in high log of odds (LOD) score families associated two haplotypes (H21N1 and H21N2) in 21q22 with neuroticism. Furthermore, two loci on chromosome 11 (11p14 and 11q23) and one locus on chromosome 10, overlap with previous findings on neuroticism (Cloninger et al., 1998; Fullerton et al., 2003; Kuo et al., 2007; Neale et al., 2005). However, taken together, all these studies provide few replications and when a linkage region with anxiety-related traits is detected, the effect size is small or at least moderate.

To date, a number of GWASs have been published, but they have failed to identify any locus with genome-wide significance (Luciano et al., 2012; Shifman et al., 2008; Terracciano et al., 2010; Verweij et al., 2010). Moreover, a lack of association has been also shown from GWAS meta-analyses (de Moor et al., 2012; Service et al., 2012).

Two GWASs have respectively suggested a potential association between variants in MAM domain-containing glycosylphosphatidylinositol anchor protein 2 (MAMDC1) and olfactory receptor 1A2 (ORIA2) genes with neuroticism (Kim et al., 2013; van den Oord et al., 2008), with contrasting replication findings (Calboli et al., 2010; Heck et al., 2011; Kim et al., 2013; Terracciano et al., 2010).

The dilemma of moderate-to-high heritability, of which only a small proportion can be explained by markers, has been expressed as "the case of the missing heritability" (Manolio et al., 2009). Proposed explanations focus on: many variants of very small effect that are yet to be found; rare variants that are poorly detected by available genotyping arrays that focus on variants present in at least 5% of the population; structural variants poorly captured by existing arrays, such as CNVs; and low power to detect epistasis (interaction between genes) (Manolio et al., 2009). Newer technologies (e.g., whole-genome sequencing) and novel statistical approaches, combined with larger samples and meta-analyses, will contribute to the understanding of the genetic architecture of complex traits.

A novel statistical approach is represented by polygenic analysis studies. With this approach, a recent study (Vinkhuyzen et al., 2012) has shown that common SNPs explain 6% of the phenotypic variance for neuroticism. These results suggest a polygenic model in which a large number of variants individually explain a small proportion of the variance.

Anxiety Disorders Treatment Outcome: Pharmacogenetic and Therapygenetic Studies

Antidepressant drugs are the cornerstone of pharmacotherapy of various anxiety disorders. In particular, selective serotonin reuptake inhibitors (SSRIs) are recommended in PD, GAD, social phobia, PTSD and OCD, and their efficacy has been shown in a large number of controlled studies. Furthermore, serotonin and noradrenaline reuptake inhibitors (SNRIs) and tricyclic antidepressants have demonstrated a good efficacy. In addition, benzodiazepines are still widely used for the treatment of several anxiety disorders (Bandelow et al., 2012). The identification of predictive biomarkers of response to pharmacological treatment in anxiety disorders could be useful for the optimization of therapies, to decrease the wide variability in patients' clinical response, and consequently reduce the high social and economic costs related to these disorders. Pharmacogenetic research focuses on the identification of genetic variants that predict which individuals may optimally benefit from certain drug treatments and/or reduce the likelihood of their adverse effects.

To date, just a few pharmacogenetic studies have focused on antidepressant treatment response in anxiety disorders. Even in this field, the most studied has been the 5-HTTLPR. Some studies have showed evidence for a significant influence of 5-HTTLPR variants on response to SSRIs in PD, as well as in social phobia (Perna et al., 2005; Saeki et al., 2009; Stein et al., 2006). Furthermore, there is evidence regarding an involvement of variants in the serotonin receptor genes (5-HT1A and 5-HT2A) in antidepressant response in PD, GAD and OCD (Denys et al., 2007; Ishiguro et al., 2011; Lohoff et al., 2013; Yevtushenko et al., 2010). Inconclusive results have been instead found for COMT, BDNF, MAO-A and dopamine-related gene polymorphisms (Schosser and Kasper, 2009).

Although the first-line treatment for anxiety disorders is represented by antidepressant drugs, cognitive behavioral therapy (CBT) is an effective treatment, recommended by treatment guidelines. As for pharmacotherapy, also for CBT many patients do not respond sufficiently. Therefore, the opportunity to select which patients could respond to CBT and to optimize the efficacy of the treatment would be relevant. Recently, genetic studies are addressing on the outcome of psychological treatments, the so-called "therapygenetics studies". However, despite the expanding of this field, there has been just a handful of papers testing for associations between specific genetic markers and response to psychological therapy for anxiety disorders. Regarding 5-HTTLPR, results are still contrasting: one study has found that who possesses the S allele has less probability to respond well to CBT (Bryant et al., 2010), but several have shown no effect at all (Bockting et al., 2013; Hedman et al., 2012; Hudson et al., 2013; Lonsdorf et al., 2010), though it should be noted that the precise disorder, treatment and sample size in these studies vary quite considerably. Several other markers have also been considered as predictors of psychological treatment response, including variants in the COMT (Hedman et al., 2012; Lonsdorf et al., 2010), MAO-A (Reif et al., 2013), nerve growth factor (NGF) (Hudson et al., 2013; Lester et al., 2012) and BDNF genes (Fullana et al., 2012; Hedman et al., 2012; Lester et al., 2012).

EPIGENETIC STUDIES

The term "epigenetics" refers to long-lasting changes in gene expression which cannot be accounted for by changes in DNA sequence and can be influenced by the environment. These include DNA methylation, acetylation and histone modifications, which can alter DNA accessibility and chromatine structure. Preclinical studies have highlighted how environmental stressors can induce epigenetic modifications in the brain (Heinzelmann and Gill, 2013; Tardito et al., 2013). In particular, it has been documented that early life stress can have an impact on stress response through epigenetic programming. In rats, maternal care has been shown to induce long-lasting epigenetic effects on the offspring: indeed, poorer caregiving has been associated with an anxious phenotype, higher corticosterone levels in response to stress and alterations in DNA methylation and histone acetylation. Although these alterations last in the adulthood, they are potentially reversible (Weaver et al., 2004; Weaver et al., 2006). Also maternal separation in mice has been described to induce epigenetic changes, consisting in hypomethylation in the AVP gene enhancer region, leading to an increase in hypothalamic AVP expression, accompanied by enhanced corticosterone secretion (Murgatroyd et al., 2009). Finally, in the prefrontal cortex (PFC) of adult rats subjected to early life maltreatment, an increased methylation in BDNF-4 and BDNF-9 exons has been reported, leading to reduced levels of BDNF mRNA levels (Roth et al., 2009). Recent research has involved epigenetic mechanisms also in the pathophysiology of many psychiatric disorders, including anxiety disorders, in particular PTSD. Studies in chronic PTSD patients reported hypermethylation of proinflammatory genes (such as toll-like receptors 1 and 3, interleukin 8, chemokine ligand 1) and hypomethylation of inflammation regulatory genes (such as FKBP5) (Uddin et al., 2010). Also differential methylation of neurotransmitter genes has been described in PTSD. The serotonin transporter (SLC6A4) methylation levels have been shown to be modified by the effect of the number of traumatic events, after controlling for SLC6A4 genotype. Individuals with more traumatic events were at increased risk for PTSD, but only at lower methylation levels. At higher methylation levels, individuals who reported more traumatic events were protected, suggesting that this gene may be also important in trauma-related resilience (Koenen et al., 2011). On these bases, the traditional gene-environment model, describing the interaction of genetic background and environmental factors (comprising adverse life events and stress) in determining a given phenotype, should be integrated in an epigenetic perspective, recognizing the role played by previous environmental effects on the epigenome (Tardito et al., 2013).

CONCLUSION

To date, it is not yet clear whether there are common biological mechanisms shared between different anxiety disorders or biological mechanisms that indicate their specificity. With the genetic association data now available, it is difficult to achieve conclusive findings, mainly because of the large heterogeneity between studies. In particular, several different genes have been often studied in different anxiety disorders, without a within comparison. Furthermore, the samples studied often show heterogeneity in diagnosis, ethnicity, sample size, and so on. Therefore, the use of endophenotypes becomes increasingly important.

Generally speaking, although for some genes an association has been found across different anxiety disorders, the above-reported genetic data suggest the distinction of three main groups of anxiety disorders: 1) PD and similar disorders, such as phobias and GAD; 2) OCD; 3) PTSD. In relation to this issue, in the new DSM-5 the chapter on anxiety disorders no longer includes OCD (which is included with the obsessive-compulsive and related disorders) and PTSD (which is included with the trauma- and stressor-related disorders).

With the currently available genetic data, it is still difficult to understand whether there are common biological mechanisms shared between anxiety disorders and other disorders, such as MDD, that often occur in comorbity.

Furthermore, it is still difficult to clarify the results which indicate a common mechanism, such as the involvement of the HPA axis in MDD and anxiety disorders, since studies are often affected by design biases, due to the presence of anxiety disorders in comorbity. In order to stimulate a greater specificity and consequently improve the diagnosis, treatment, epidemiologic data and the study of the possible underlying neurobiological mechanisms, the DSM-5 suggests to clinicians and researchers a greater awareness about the importance of assessing anxiety in presence of mood symptoms.

Although the pharmacogenetics and therapygenetics studies are in an early discovery phase, these approaches have the potential to aid clinicians when selecting appropriate treatments for their patients. Data from these studies could be used to predict treatment outcomes and thus contribute to stratified medicine, identifying groups of individuals showing a similar treatment-response. Finally, these studies will improve the understanding of the mechanisms by which genetic factors influence response to drugs and to environmental experiences, such as psychological treatments.

Although no robust genetic finding has to date emerged, it is plausible that the application of modern molecular genetic methods and multicentric collaborations bringing together large well-characterized samples, will help to identify susceptibility genes for anxiety disorders and treatment response. In particular, the developments in large-scale genome-wide association studies, whole genome sequencing, copy number variants, epigenetic and gene expression analyses will soon allow for convergent genomic approaches to define gene pathways critically involved in anxiety disorders.

Acknowledgments

We would like to express sincere gratitude to our supervisor Prof. Massimo Gennarelli for his precious support.

References

Almli LM, Fani N, Smith AK, Ressler KJ (2013). Genetic approaches to understanding post-traumatic stress disorder. *Int J Neuropsychopharmacol*, 1-16.

Amin N, Schuur M, Gusareva ES, Isaacs A *et al.* (2012). A genome-wide linkage study of individuals with high scores on NEO personality traits. *Mol Psychiatry* 17, 1031-1041.

Amstadter AB, Nugent NR, Yang BZ, Miller A *et al.* (2011). Corticotrophin-releasing hormone type 1 receptor gene (CRHR1) variants predict posttraumatic stress disorder onset and course in pediatric injury patients. *Dis Markers* 30, 89-99.

Andre K, Kampman O, Viikki M, Illi A *et al.* (2013). TPH1 A218C polymorphism and temperament in major depression. *BMC Psychiatry* 13, 118.

Arnold PD, Sicard T, Burroughs E, Richter MA *et al.* (2006). Glutamate transporter gene SLC1A1 associated with obsessive-compulsive disorder. *Arch Gen Psychiatry* 63, 769-776.

Bandelow B, Sher L, Bunevicius R, Hollander E *et al.* (2012). Guidelines for the pharmacological treatment of anxiety disorders, obsessive-compulsive disorder and posttraumatic stress disorder in primary care. *Int J Psychiatry Clin Pract* 16, 77-84.

Bengel D, Greenberg BD, Cora-Locatelli G, Altemus M *et al.* (1999). Association of the serotonin transporter promoter regulatory region polymorphism and obsessive-compulsive disorder. *Mol Psychiatry* 4, 463-466.

Binder EB (2009). The role of FKBP5, a co-chaperone of the glucocorticoid receptor in the pathogenesis and therapy of affective and anxiety disorders. *Psychoneuroendocrinology* 34 Suppl 1, S186-195.

Blaya C, Salum GA, Moorjani P, Seganfredo AC *et al.* (2010). Panic disorder and serotonergic genes (SLC6A4, HTR1A and HTR2A): Association and interaction with childhood trauma and parenting. *Neurosci Lett* 485, 11-15.

Bockting CL, Mocking RJ, Lok A, Koeter MW *et al.* (2013). Therapygenetics: the 5HTTLPR as a biomarker for response to psychological therapy? *Mol Psychiatry* 18, 744-745.

Bonfiglio JJ, Inda C, Refojo D, Holsboer F *et al.* (2011). The corticotropin-releasing hormone network and the hypothalamic-pituitary-adrenal axis: molecular and cellular mechanisms involved. *Neuroendocrinology* 94, 12-20.

Bouchard TJ, Jr. and Loehlin JC (2001). Genes, evolution, and personality. *Behav Genet* 31, 243-273.

Brandes M and Bienvenu OJ (2006). Personality and anxiety disorders. *Curr Psychiatry Rep* 8, 263-269.

Bryant RA, Felmingham KL, Falconer EM, Pe Benito L *et al.* (2010). Preliminary evidence of the short allele of the serotonin transporter gene predicting poor response to cognitive behavior therapy in posttraumatic stress disorder. *Biol Psychiatry* 67, 1217-1219.

Calboli FC, Tozzi F, Galwey NW, Antoniades A *et al.* (2010). A genome-wide association study of neuroticism in a population-based sample. *PLoS One* 5, e11504.

Choe AY, Kim B, Lee KS, Lee JE *et al.* (2013). Serotonergic genes (5-HTT and HTR1A) and separation life events: gene-by-environment interaction for panic disorder. *Neuropsychobiology* 67, 192-200.

Cloninger CR, Svrakic DM, Przybeck TR (1993). A psychobiological model of temperament and character. *Arch Gen Psychiatry* 50, 975-990.

Cloninger CR, Van Eerdewegh P, Goate A, Edenberg HJ *et al.* (1998). Anxiety proneness linked to epistatic loci in genome scan of human personality traits. *Am J Med Genet* 81, 313-317.

Cotton CH, Flint J, Campbell TG (2009). Is there an association between NPY and neuroticism? *Nature* 458, E6; discussion E7.

Craske MG, Rauch SL, Ursano R, Prenoveau J *et al.* (2009). What is an anxiety disorder? *Depress Anxiety* 26, 1066-1085.

Crowe RR, Goedken R, Samuelson S, Wilson R *et al.* (2001). Genomewide survey of panic disorder. *Am J Med Genet* 105, 105-109.

De Fruyt F, De Clercq BJ, van de Wiele L, Van Heeringen K (2006). The validity of Cloninger's psychobiological model versus the five-factor model to predict DSM-IV personality disorders in a heterogeneous psychiatric sample: domain facet and residualized facet descriptions. *J Pers* 74, 479-510.

de Moor MH, Costa PT, Terracciano A, Krueger RF *et al.* (2012). Meta-analysis of genome-wide association studies for personality. *Mol Psychiatry* 17, 337-349.

Denys D, Van Nieuwerburgh F, Deforce D, Westenberg HG (2007). Prediction of response to paroxetine and venlafaxine by serotonin-related genes in obsessive-compulsive disorder in a randomized, double-blind trial. *J Clin Psychiatry* 68, 747-753.

Dickel DE, Veenstra-VanderWeele J, Cox NJ, Wu X *et al.* (2006). Association testing of the positional and functional candidate gene SLC1A1/EAAC1 in early-onset obsessive-compulsive disorder. *Arch Gen Psychiatry* 63, 778-785.

Digangi J, Guffanti G, McLaughlin KA, Koenen KC (2013). Considering trauma exposure in the context of genetics studies of posttraumatic stress disorder: a systematic review. *Biol Mood Anxiety Disord* 3, 2.

Domschke K and Deckert J (2012). Genetics Of Anxiety Disorders Status Quo And Quo Vadis. *Curr Pharm Des.*

Domschke K, Deckert J, O'Donovan M C, Glatt SJ (2007). Meta-analysis of COMT val158met in panic disorder: ethnic heterogeneity and gender specificity. *Am J Med Genet B Neuropsychiatr Genet* 144B, 667-673.

Domschke K, Freitag CM, Kuhlenbaumer G, Schirmacher A *et al.* (2004). Association of the functional V158M catechol-O-methyl-transferase polymorphism with panic disorder in women. *Int J Neuropsychopharmacol* 7, 183-188.

Domschke K, Tidow N, Kuithan H, Schwarte K *et al.* (2012). Monoamine oxidase A gene DNA hypomethylation - a risk factor for panic disorder? *Int J Neuropsychopharmacol* 15, 1217-1228.

Erhardt A, Akula N, Schumacher J, Czamara D *et al.* (2012). Replication and meta-analysis of TMEM132D gene variants in panic disorder. *Transl Psychiatry* 2, e156.

Erhardt A, Czibere L, Roeske D, Lucae S *et al.* (2011). TMEM132D, a new candidate for anxiety phenotypes: evidence from human and mouse studies. *Mol Psychiatry* 16, 647-663.

Faludi G, Gonda X, Bagdy G, Dome P (2012). Pharmaco- and therapygenetic aspects in the treatment of anxiety disorders beyond the serotonergic system: a brief review. *Neuropsychopharmacol Hung* 14, 221-229.

Fava M, Rankin MA, Wright EC, Alpert JE *et al.* (2000). Anxiety disorders in major depression. *Compr Psychiatry* 41, 97-102.

Fava M, Rush AJ, Alpert JE, Balasubramani GK *et al.* (2008). Difference in treatment outcome in outpatients with anxious versus nonanxious depression: a STAR*D report. *Am J Psychiatry* 165, 342-351.

Fiori LM and Turecki G (2008). Implication of the polyamine system in mental disorders. *J Psychiatry Neurosci* 33, 102-110.

Fox JH and Lowry CA (2013). Corticotropin-releasing factor-related peptides, serotonergic systems, and emotional behavior. *Front Neurosci* 7, 169.

Fullana MA, Alonso P, Gratacos M, Jaurrieta N *et al.* (2012). Variation in the BDNF Val66Met polymorphism and response to cognitive-behavior therapy in obsessive-compulsive disorder. *Eur Psychiatry* 27, 386-390.

Fullerton J, Cubin M, Tiwari H, Wang C *et al.* (2003). Linkage analysis of extremely discordant and concordant sibling pairs identifies quantitative-trait loci that influence variation in the human personality trait neuroticism. *Am J Hum Genet* 72, 879-890.

Fyer AJ, Hamilton SP, Durner M, Haghighi F *et al.* (2006). A third-pass genome scan in panic disorder: evidence for multiple susceptibility loci. *Biol Psychiatry* 60, 388-401.

Gelernter J, Bonvicini K, Page G, Woods SW *et al.* (2001). Linkage genome scan for loci predisposing to panic disorder or agoraphobia. *Am J Med Genet* 105, 548-557.

Gillespie NA, Zhu G, Evans DM, Medland SE *et al.* (2008). A genome-wide scan for Eysenckian personality dimensions in adolescent twin sibships: psychoticism, extraversion, neuroticism, and lie. *J Pers* 76, 1415-1446.

Gottesman, II and Gould TD (2003). The endophenotype concept in psychiatry: etymology and strategic intentions. *Am J Psychiatry* 160, 636-645.

Gregersen N, Dahl HA, Buttenschon HN, Nyegaard M *et al.* (2012). A genome-wide study of panic disorder suggests the amiloride-sensitive cation channel 1 as a candidate gene. *Eur J Hum Genet* 20, 84-90.

Gressier F, Calati R, Balestri M, Marsano A *et al.* (2013). The 5-HTTLPR Polymorphism and Posttraumatic Stress Disorder: A Meta-Analysis. *J Trauma Stress.*

Hamilton SP, Fyer AJ, Durner M, Heiman GA *et al.* (2003). Further genetic evidence for a panic disorder syndrome mapping to chromosome 13q. *Proc Natl Acad Sci U S A* 100, 2550-2555.

Hamilton SP, Slager SL, De Leon AB, Heiman GA *et al.* (2004). Evidence for genetic linkage between a polymorphism in the adenosine 2A receptor and panic disorder. *Neuropsychopharmacology* 29, 558-565.

Heath AC, Cloninger CR, Martin NG (1994). Testing a model for the genetic structure of personality: a comparison of the personality systems of Cloninger and Eysenck. *J Pers Soc Psychol* 66, 762-775.

Heck A, Pfister H, Czamara D, Muller-Myhsok B *et al.* (2011). Evidence for associations between MDGA2 polymorphisms and harm avoidance: replication and extension of a genome-wide association finding. *Psychiatr Genet* 21, 257-260.

Hedman E, Andersson E, Ljotsson B, Andersson G *et al.* (2012). Clinical and genetic outcome determinants of Internet- and group-based cognitive behavior therapy for social anxiety disorder. *Acta Psychiatr Scand* 126, 126-136.

Heinzelmann M and Gill J (2013). Epigenetic Mechanisms Shape the Biological Response to Trauma and Risk for PTSD: A Critical Review. *Nurs Res Pract* 2013, 417010.

Hohoff C, Mullings EL, Heatherley SV, Freitag CM *et al.* (2010). Adenosine A(2A) receptor gene: evidence for association of risk variants with panic disorder and anxious personality. *J Psychiatr Res* 44, 930-937.

Hosing VG, Schirmacher A, Kuhlenbaumer G, Freitag C *et al.* (2004). Cholecystokinin- and cholecystokinin-B-receptor gene polymorphisms in panic disorder. *J Neural Transm Suppl*, 147-156.

Hu XZ, Lipsky RH, Zhu G, Akhtar LA *et al.* (2006). Serotonin transporter promoter gain-of-function genotypes are linked to obsessive-compulsive disorder. *Am J Hum Genet* 78, 815-826.

Hudson JL, Lester KJ, Lewis CM, Tropeano M *et al.* (2013). Predicting outcomes following cognitive behaviour therapy in child anxiety disorders: the influence of genetic, demographic and clinical information. *J Child Psychol Psychiatry* 54, 1086-1094.

Hunnerkopf R, Strobel A, Gutknecht L, Brocke B *et al.* (2007). Interaction between BDNF Val66Met and dopamine transporter gene variation influences anxiety-related traits. *Neuropsychopharmacology* 32, 2552-2560.

Inada Y, Yoneda H, Koh J, Sakai J *et al.* (2003). Positive association between panic disorder and polymorphism of the serotonin 2A receptor gene. *Psychiatry Res* 118, 25-31.

Ishiguro S, Watanabe T, Ueda M, Saeki Y *et al.* (2011). Determinants of pharmacodynamic trajectory of the therapeutic response to paroxetine in Japanese patients with panic disorder. *Eur J Clin Pharmacol* 67, 1213-1221.

Juhasz G, Chase D, Pegg E, Downey D *et al.* (2009). CNR1 gene is associated with high neuroticism and low agreeableness and interacts with recent negative life events to predict current depressive symptoms. *Neuropsychopharmacology* 34, 2019-2027.

Kaabi B, Gelernter J, Woods SW, Goddard A *et al.* (2006). Genome scan for loci predisposing to anxiety disorders using a novel multivariate approach: strong evidence for a chromosome 4 risk locus. *Am J Hum Genet* 78, 543-553.

Karacetin G, Bayoglu B, Cengiz M, Demir T *et al.* (2012). Serotonin-2A receptor and catechol-O-methyltransferase polymorphisms in panic disorder. *Prog Neuropsychopharmacol Biol Psychiatry* 36, 5-10.

Kendler KS, Neale MC, Kessler RC, Heath AC *et al.* (1993). A longitudinal twin study of personality and major depression in women. *Arch Gen Psychiatry* 50, 853-862.

Kim HN, Roh SJ, Sung YA, Chung HW *et al.* (2013). Genome-wide association study of the five-factor model of personality in young Korean women. *J Hum Genet* 58, 667-674.

Klengel T, Mehta D, Anacker C, Rex-Haffner M *et al.* (2013). Allele-specific FKBP5 DNA demethylation mediates gene-childhood trauma interactions. *Nat Neurosci* 16, 33-41.

Knowles JA, Fyer AJ, Vieland VJ, Weissman MM *et al.* (1998). Results of a genome-wide genetic screen for panic disorder. *Am J Med Genet* 81, 139-147.

Koenen KC, Uddin M, Chang SC, Aiello AE *et al.* (2011). SLC6A4 methylation modifies the effect of the number of traumatic events on risk for posttraumatic stress disorder. *Depress Anxiety* 28, 639-647.

Kuo PH, Neale MC, Riley BP, Patterson DG *et al.* (2007). A genome-wide linkage analysis for the personality trait neuroticism in the Irish affected sib-pair study of alcohol dependence. *Am J Med Genet B Neuropsychiatr Genet* 144B, 463-468.

LeBeau RT, Glenn D, Liao B, Wittchen HU *et al.* (2010). Specific phobia: a review of DSM-IV specific phobia and preliminary recommendations for DSM-V. *Depress Anxiety* 27, 148-167.

Lesch KP, Bengel D, Heils A, Sabol SZ *et al.* (1996). Association of anxiety-related traits with a polymorphism in the serotonin transporter gene regulatory region. *Science* 274, 1527-1531.

Lester KJ, Hudson JL, Tropeano M, Creswell C *et al.* (2012). Neurotrophic gene polymorphisms and response to psychological therapy. *Transl Psychiatry* 2, e108.

Logue MW, Baldwin C, Guffanti G, Melista E *et al.* (2013). A genome-wide association study of post-traumatic stress disorder identifies the retinoid-related orphan receptor alpha (RORA) gene as a significant risk locus. *Mol Psychiatry* 18, 937-942.

Lohoff FW, Aquino TD, Narasimhan S, Multani PK *et al.* (2013). Serotonin receptor 2A (HTR2A) gene polymorphism predicts treatment response to venlafaxine XR in generalized anxiety disorder. *Pharmacogenomics J* 13, 21-26.

Lonsdorf TB, Ruck C, Bergstrom J, Andersson G *et al.* (2010). The COMTval158met polymorphism is associated with symptom relief during exposure-based cognitive-behavioral treatment in panic disorder. *BMC Psychiatry* 10, 99.

Luciano M, Huffman JE, Arias-Vasquez A, Vinkhuyzen AA *et al.* (2012). Genome-wide association uncovers shared genetic effects among personality traits and mood states. *Am J Med Genet B Neuropsychiatr Genet* 159B, 684-695.

Manolio TA, Collins FS, Cox NJ, Goldstein DB *et al.* (2009). Finding the missing heritability of complex diseases. *Nature* 461, 747-753.

Maser JD and Cloninger CR (1990). Comorbidity of mood and Anxiety Disorders. Washington DC: American Psychiatric Press.

Mehta D, Gonik M, Klengel T, Rex-Haffner M *et al.* (2011). Using polymorphisms in FKBP5 to define biologically distinct subtypes of posttraumatic stress disorder: evidence from endocrine and gene expression studies. *Arch Gen Psychiatry* 68, 901-910.

Minelli A, Bonvicini C, Scassellati C, Sartori R *et al.* (2011a). The influence of psychiatric screening in healthy populations selection: A new study and meta-analysis of functional 5-HTTLPR and rs25531 polymorphisms and anxiety-related personality traits. *BMC Psychiatry* 11.

Minelli A, Maffioletti E, Cloninger CR, Magri C *et al.* (2013). Role of allelic variants of FK506-binding protein 51 (fkbp5) gene in the development of anxiety disorders. *Depress Anxiety* 30, 1170-1176.

Minelli A, Scassellati C, Bonvicini C, Perez J *et al.* (2009). An association of GRIK3 Ser310Ala functional polymorphism with personality traits. *Neuropsychobiology* 59, 28-33.

Minelli A, Zanardini R, Bonvicini C, Sartori R *et al.* (2011b). BDNF serum levels, but not BDNF Val66Met genotype, are correlated with personality traits in healthy subjects. *Eur Arch Psychiatry Clin Neurosci* 261, 323-329.

Miyasaka K, Yoshida Y, Matsushita S, Higuchi S *et al.* (2004). Association of cholecystokinin-A receptor gene polymorphisms and panic disorder in Japanese. *Am J Med Genet B Neuropsychiatr Genet* 127B, 78-80.

Mohler H (2012). The GABA system in anxiety and depression and its therapeutic potential. *Neuropharmacology* 62, 42-53.

Murgatroyd C, Patchev AV, Wu Y, Micale V *et al.* (2009). Dynamic DNA methylation programs persistent adverse effects of early-life stress. *Nat Neurosci* 12, 1559-1566.

Murphy DL, Maile MS, Vogt NM (2013a). 5HTTLPR: White Knight or Dark Blight? *ACS Chem Neurosci* 4, 13-15.

Murphy DL, Moya PR, Fox MA, Rubenstein LM *et al.* (2013b). Anxiety and affective disorder comorbidity related to serotonin and other neurotransmitter systems: obsessive-compulsive disorder as an example of overlapping clinical and genetic heterogeneity. *Philos Trans R Soc Lond B Biol Sci* 368, 20120435.

Nash MW, Huezo-Diaz P, Williamson RJ, Sterne A *et al.* (2004). Genome-wide linkage analysis of a composite index of neuroticism and mood-related scales in extreme selected sibships. *Hum Mol Genet* 13, 2173-2182.

Nash MW, Sugden K, Huezo-Diaz P, Williamson R *et al.* (2005). Association analysis of monoamine genes with measures of depression and anxiety in a selected community sample of siblings. *Am J Med Genet B Neuropsychiatr Genet* 135B, 33-37.

Neale BM, Sullivan PF, Kendler KS (2005). A genome scan of neuroticism in nicotine dependent smokers. *Am J Med Genet B Neuropsychiatr Genet* 132B, 65-69.

Otowa T, Kawamura Y, Nishida N, Sugaya N *et al.* (2012). Meta-analysis of genome-wide association studies for panic disorder in the Japanese population. *Transl Psychiatry* 2, e186.

Paterson AD, Sunohara GA, Kennedy JL (1999). Dopamine D4 receptor gene: novelty or nonsense? *Neuropsychopharmacology* 21, 3-16.

Perna G, Favaron E, Di Bella D, Bussi R *et al.* (2005). Antipanic efficacy of paroxetine and polymorphism within the promoter of the serotonin transporter gene. *Neuropsychopharmacology* 30, 2230-2235.

Reif A, Richter J, Straube B, Hofler M *et al.* (2013). MAOA and mechanisms of panic disorder revisited: from bench to molecular psychotherapy. *Mol Psychiatry.*

Reif A, Weber H, Domschke K, Klauke B *et al.* (2012). Meta-analysis argues for a female-specific role of MAOA-uVNTR in panic disorder in four European populations. *Am J Med Genet B Neuropsychiatr Genet* 159B, 786-793.

Riaza Bermudo-Soriano C, Perez-Rodriguez MM, Vaquero-Lorenzo C, Baca-Garcia E (2012). New perspectives in glutamate and anxiety. *Pharmacol Biochem Behav* 100, 752-774.

Roth TL, Lubin FD, Funk AJ, Sweatt JD (2009). Lasting epigenetic influence of early-life adversity on the BDNF gene. *Biol Psychiatry* 65, 760-769.

Saeki Y, Watanabe T, Ueda M, Saito A *et al.* (2009). Genetic and pharmacokinetic factors affecting the initial pharmacotherapeutic effect of paroxetine in Japanese patients with panic disorder. *Eur J Clin Pharmacol* 65, 685-691.

Samochowiec J, Hajduk A, Samochowiec A, Horodnicki J *et al.* (2004). Association studies of MAO-A, COMT, and 5-HTT genes polymorphisms in patients with anxiety disorders of the phobic spectrum. *Psychiatry Res* 128, 21-26.

Sarapas C, Cai G, Bierer LM, Golier JA *et al.* (2011). Genetic markers for PTSD risk and resilience among survivors of the World Trade Center attacks. *Dis Markers* 30, 101-110.

Schosser A and Kasper S (2009). The role of pharmacogenetics in the treatment of depression and anxiety disorders. *Int Clin Psychopharmacol* 24, 277-288.

Service SK, Verweij KJ, Lahti J, Congdon E *et al.* (2012). A genome-wide meta-analysis of association studies of Cloninger's Temperament Scales. *Transl Psychiatry* 2, e116.

Shear MK, Bjelland I, Beesdo K, Gloster AT *et al.* (2007). Supplementary dimensional assessment in anxiety disorders. *Int J Methods Psychiatr Res* 16 Suppl 1, S52-64.

Shibuya N, Suzuki A, Sadahiro R, Kamata M *et al.* (2010). Association study between a functional polymorphism of FK506-binding protein 51 (FKBP5) gene and personality traits in healthy subjects. *Neurosci Lett* 485, 194-197.

Shifman S, Bhomra A, Smiley S, Wray NR *et al.* (2008). A whole genome association study of neuroticism using DNA pooling. *Mol Psychiatry* 13, 302-312.

Shugart YY, Wang Y, Samuels JF, Grados MA *et al.* (2009). A family-based association study of the glutamate transporter gene SLC1A1 in obsessive-compulsive disorder in 378 families. *Am J Med Genet B Neuropsychiatr Genet* 150B, 886-892.

Stein MB, Seedat S, Gelernter J (2006). Serotonin transporter gene promoter polymorphism predicts SSRI response in generalized social anxiety disorder. *Psychopharmacology (Berl)* 187, 68-72.

Stewart SE, Fagerness JA, Platko J, Smoller JW *et al.* (2007). Association of the SLC1A1 glutamate transporter gene and obsessive-compulsive disorder. *Am J Med Genet B Neuropsychiatr Genet* 144B, 1027-1033.

Stewart SE Yu D Scharf JM Neale BM *et al.* (2013). Genome-wide association study of obsessive-compulsive disorder. *Mol Psychiatry* 18, 788-798.

Szekely A, Ronai Z, Nemoda Z, Kolmann G *et al.* (2004). Human personality dimensions of persistence and harm avoidance associated with DRD4 and 5-HTTLPR polymorphisms. *Am J Med Genet B Neuropsychiatr Genet* 126B, 106-110.

Tardito D, Mallei A, Popoli M (2013). Lost in translation. New unexplored avenues for neuropsychopharmacology: epigenetics and microRNAs. *Expert Opin Investig Drugs* 22, 217-233.

Terracciano A, Sanna S, Uda M, Deiana B *et al.* (2010). Genome-wide association scan for five major dimensions of personality. *Mol Psychiatry* 15, 647-656.

Thorgeirsson TE, Oskarsson H, Desnica N, Kostic JP *et al.* (2003). Anxiety with panic disorder linked to chromosome 9q in Iceland. *Am J Hum Genet* 72, 1221-1230.

Uddin M, Aiello AE, Wildman DE, Koenen KC *et al.* (2010). Epigenetic and immune function profiles associated with posttraumatic stress disorder. *Proc Natl Acad Sci U S A* 107, 9470-9475.

van den Oord EJ, Kuo PH, Hartmann AM, Webb BT *et al.* (2008). Genomewide association analysis followed by a replication study implicates a novel candidate gene for neuroticism. *Arch Gen Psychiatry* 65, 1062-1071.

Verweij KJ, Zietsch BP, Medland SE, Gordon SD *et al.* (2010). A genome-wide association study of Cloninger's temperament scales: implications for the evolutionary genetics of personality. *Biol Psychol* 85, 306-317.

Vinkhuyzen AA, Pedersen NL, Yang J, Lee SH *et al.* (2012). Common SNPs explain some of the variation in the personality dimensions of neuroticism and extraversion. *Transl Psychiatry* 2, e102.

Wang Y, Adamczyk A, Shugart YY, Samuels JF *et al.* (2010). A screen of SLC1A1 for OCD-related alleles. *Am J Med Genet B Neuropsychiatr Genet* 153B, 675-679.

Weaver IC, Cervoni N, Champagne FA, D'Alessio AC *et al.* (2004). Epigenetic programming by maternal behavior. *Nat Neurosci* 7, 847-854.

Weaver IC, Meaney MJ, Szyf M (2006). Maternal care effects on the hippocampal transcriptome and anxiety-mediated behaviors in the offspring that are reversible in adulthood. *Proc Natl Acad Sci U S A* 103, 3480-3485.

Weber H, Scholz CJ, Domschke K, Baumann C *et al.* (2012). Gender differences in associations of glutamate decarboxylase 1 gene (GAD1) variants with panic disorder. *PLoS One* 7, e37651.

Wendland JR, Moya PR, Kruse MR, Ren-Patterson RF *et al.* (2008). A novel, putative gain-of-function haplotype at SLC6A4 associates with obsessive-compulsive disorder. *Hum Mol Genet* 17, 717-723.

White S, Acierno R, Ruggiero KJ, Koenen KC *et al.* (2013). Association of CRHR1 variants and posttraumatic stress symptoms in hurricane exposed adults. *J Anxiety Disord* 27, 678-683.

Wray NR, Middeldorp CM, Birley AJ, Gordon SD *et al.* (2008). Genome-wide linkage analysis of multiple measures of neuroticism of 2 large cohorts from Australia and the Netherlands. *Arch Gen Psychiatry* 65, 649-658.

Yevtushenko OO, Oros MM, Reynolds GP (2010). Early response to selective serotonin reuptake inhibitors in panic disorder is associated with a functional 5-HT1A receptor gene polymorphism. *J Affect Disord* 123, 308-311.

Zhou Z, Zhu G, Hariri AR, Enoch MA *et al.* (2008). Genetic variation in human NPY expression affects stress response and emotion. *Nature* 452, 997-1001.

Zuckerman M and Cloninger CR (1996). Relationships between Cloninger's, Zuckerman's, and Eysenck's dimension of personality. *Pers Individ Differ* 21, 283-285.

In: Anxiety Disorders
Editor: Shiloh Angelus Roman
ISBN: 978-1-63117-392-9

Chapter 4

ANXIETY AND TEMPOROMANDIBULAR DISORDERS: A RELATIONSHIP IN CHRONIC PAIN DEVELOPMENT

***Tomislav Badel, D.M.D., Ph.D.,*[*1]**
***Sandra Kocijan Lovko, M.D., M.Sc.,*[2]**
***and Dijana Zadravec, Ph.D.*[3]**
[1]Department of Removable Prosthodontics,
School of Dental Medicine, University of Zagreb, Zagreb, Croatia
[2]"Vrapče Psychiatry Clinic" Zagreb, Croatia
[3]Department of Diagnostic and Interventional Radiology,
Clinical Hospital Center "'Sestre Milosrdnice",
University of Zagreb, Croatia

ABSTRACT

The current decade (2010-2020), which has been dedicated to bone and joint diseases by the World Health Organization, is the right time to pay attention to musculoskeletal diseases of the orofacial system. Musculoskeletal diseases play a very important role at both the individual and the societal level, because they are generally extremely common in

* Correspondence to: Associate Prof. Tomislav Badel, PhD, Department of Removable Prosthodontics, School of Dental Medicine, University of Zagreb, Gundulićeva 5, 10 000 Zagreb, E-mail: badel@sfzg.hr.

today's world. The development of a number of musculoskeletal diseases is closely related to decreasing age and increasing longevity, and is more common in females.

Temporomandibular disorders (TMD) are arthrogenic and myogenic disorders in the area of temporomandibular joints (TMJs) and/or masticatory muscles. TMDs show a greater frequency in females, and our open longitudinal study undertaken between 2001 to 2012 confirmed these epidemiological data, i.e., that TMDs are up to four times more frequent. Their main clinical characteristic is musculoskeletal pain and they are one of the most common causes of pain in the stomatognathous system. Magnetic resonance imaging was used as a 'gold standard' tool for diagnosing intra-articular TMD. The prevalence of clinical symptoms in the adult population ranges from 12% TO 42.7% and the need for treatment, from 3% to 9%. The etiopathogenesis of TMD has not been entirely explained and it is characterized by a multifactorial etiology, with a number of mutually interacting physical and psychosocial factors. Moreover, TMD constitutes the most common cause of nondental, musculoskeletal pain in the orofacial region. The biopsychosocial conceptualization of the pain experience is found in the close connection between pain and psychosocial factors.

The relationship between the patients' psychological condition and their reaction to experiencing pain is very important, as are the pathophysiological mechanisms of chronic pain whose intensity is often independent of clinical findings. Untreated acute pain can evolve into a chronic form and become a separate illness. Psychosocial factors, as in other musculoskeletal disorders, play a dominant role and therefore the clinical and radiological findings tend to be disproportionate to the symptoms. Anxiety is the most common affective disorder and a great problem for psychiatry and general medicine. A certain degree of anxiety is normal and can serve as a warning signal of an external or internal threat and has lifesaving qualities. The negative effects of anxiety on the improvement of TMD pain complaints have not been completely explained. A psychological assessment was undertaken using Spielberger's State-Trait Anxiety Inventory (STAI) according to age and sex-related reference values.

Reversible, non-invasive therapeutic means are the recommended treatment, and dentists most often use the Michigan or stabilization splint. Other frequent options for the treatment of temporomandibular pain require a multidisciplinary approach, which may involve physical therapy and kinesiotherapy, acupuncture, non-steroidal anti-inflammatory drugs, biofeedback and psychotherapy. Anxiety plays a significant role as comorbidity with TMD-related orofacial pain. Regarding the important role of psychological factors in the development of temporomandibular pain, a system of multidisciplinary diagnosis is needed in TMJ diagnostics, such as STAI, a very easy-to-use psychological tool.

INTRODUCTION

Musculoskeletal disorders in the area of the stomatognathic system comprise the articular and/or muscular component of temporomandibular disorders (TMDs). The masticatory muscles (myogenic subgroup) and/or articular component (disc displacement and degenerative bone changes or osteoarthritis) are the most common cause of orofacial somatic nonodontogenic pain [1].

The current decade (2010-2020), which has been dedicated to bone and joint diseases by the World Health Organization, is the right time to pay attention to musculoskeletal diseases of the orofacial system [2]. On one hand, musculoskeletal structures of the stomatognathic system are beyond the scope of interest of medical management and on the other hand, as a part of dental medicine, the odontogenic causes of orofacial pain as well as changes in the oral cavity are most often observed. A third factor is the patients themselves and since they do not have adequate knowledge of temporomandibular joints, they associate the pain with other organs, such as the ear. The narrow, independent focus of medical and dental specialists and their poor interdisciplinary collaboration result in treatment of only those illnesses that are in comorbidity with, and topographic proximity to, the TMDs (for example, headaches, cervical spine ailments, etc.). In such a case unnecessary diagnostics are often performed and even incorrect treatment. All this leads to the patient suffering from TMD-related pain, which can, with a variable clinical picture, hinder the analgesic effects of treatment methods [3, 4].

This chapter aims to describe the relationship between TMDs as musculoskeletal disorders and psychological factors, with an overview of the influence of anxiety on patients gathered in the open prospective study and in selected clinical cases.

BASIC AND CLASSIC CONCEPTIONS

The masticatory or stomatognathic system is a functional unit of organs and tissues of the oral cavity and the face, which perform mastication, speech, swallowing and mimic movements. The primary diseases of the stomatognathic system are congenital and acquired disorders as well as pathological processes (fractures, inflammatory cysts, tumors) which are an indication of a structured treatment, and their clinical picture and pathology are in general clearly visible during diagnostics. Functional disorders include illnesses that are treated symptomatically regardless of the severity of the symptoms and the clinical picture. The objective of such a treatment is to remove the symptoms and improve the function without any direct or significant interference with the morphological causes of the disorder [5].

Adaptation capacity is manifested by a process of progressive adaptation (modulation), which happens when the tissue is remodelled and the tissue mass increases. Once the physiological tolerance threshold is crossed, it is no longer possible to compensate for the causes of the damage. Depending on the pathophysiological causes, certain parts of the masticatory system can fall below the lowest threshold of their structural tolerance. The decompensated functional disorder is a process of regressive adaptation or remodelling during which a loss of tissue mass occurs. TMDs are based on symptoms which appear as consequences of functional decompensation [6].

A medical concept of the diseases in which an exact cause is not known refers to them as diseases of nonspecific etiology. In order to determine an actual etiopathogenic process, a number of factors are included in this concept, giving rise to a multifactorial model. Such a concept functions better in the patient population rather than at the individual level. Due to this, regardless of the development of research in terms of genetic influence and pain neurobiology, they are termed diseases of unknown etiology. Musculoskeletal disorders comprise a whole series of nonspecific illnesses, of which osteoarthritis has great importance as a public-health issue. On the other hand, temporomandibular pain should be recognized as a very common cause of orofacial pain and be separated from the benign and pain-free TMJ symptomatology such as clicking and other sporadic joint noise [7-9].

The first TMDs were described independently of each other by Goodfriend and Steinhard in 1932. The oldest theory on the origin of TMDs is related to long-term work of the American otorhinolaryngologist Costen who connected heterogenic orofacial pain with the loss of posterior teeth. From a recent perspective, the influence of teeth, that is, occlusion on masticatory muscles and joints is certain, but the concept of Costen's syndrome as a mechanic pressure of the condyles of TMJ on the auriculotemporal nerve is not anatomically possible. However, the idea of tooth loss remains even today, that is, the notion of a disturbance in the static and dynamic relationship of teeth (occlusion) and TMD occurrence. According to the neuromuscular theory, parafunction (bruxism) is a consequence of occlusal interference which causes muscular spasm and hyperactivity. A series of other theories related muscular hyperactivity to the origin of pain (the muscular theory which excludes occlusion) and included psychological factors according to which, TMDs are considered to be psychosomatic. Psychological disorders (anxiety and depression) initiate muscular hyperactivity (parafunction), which leads to occlusal disorders. According to the psycho-physiological theory, the main cause is muscular spasm, which leads to parafunction (bruxism) and occlusal disturbance. Connecting the latter and stress (a hybrid concept according to Ramfjord and Ash) is only the beginning of incorporating various factors into the multifactorial model, which is not dominant today, either theoretically or practically [10, 11]. When the potential etiological factor is present in a relatively large number of patients, then we can discuss the risk factors for the development of the disease.

TMDs Concepts and Symptomatology

A clinical examination, along with the patient's anamnestic data, is a basic part of TMD diagnostics. The patient states the presence of subjective symptoms and the examination evaluates the objective signs and symptoms. A clinical sign can be based on any clinical finding related to TMDs.

TMD symptomatology is divided into main symptoms, which are, apart from the pain in masticatory muscles and/or TMJ, limited and painful mouth opening and pathological noise in the joints. In pathogenesis of the TMDs, pain is the most important symptom on account of which patients seek treatment and hence, the main goal of the treatment is pain removal. Whereas the accompanying diagnostic symptoms (nonspecific otological symptoms and tension headaches) are fairly nonspecific and mostly irrelevant in TMD diagnostics, the main diagnostic symptoms can have varying significance in the etiopathogenesis of individual patients [12, 13]

To make a diagnosis, the presence of at least one main clinical sign is necessary. TMD symptoms are not necessarily pathognomonic to the clinical picture and their presence does not emphatically confirm the diagnosis. Similar or equal symptoms can be related to other pathological conditions in region of the face and jaw such as traumas, tumors, rheumatic diseases, headaches, and infections, among others. The secondary diagnostic symptoms are often quite nonspecific (apart from headaches) and seen individually they are mostly irrelevant in making the diagnosis [14].

TMDs do not include only one diagnostic category in a specific individual case. Based on the signs, several diagnoses from the TMDs subgroups could be made in the same patient, because one certain diagnostic subgroup does not exclude the other. Myofascial pain is most frequently included in the clinical picture, followed by arthrogenic TMD symptoms [15]. In the primary stage, TMDs can be of inflammatory or degenerative character, which is an accompanying or consequential occurrence in the further course of the pathological process. Considering the most pronounced sign and symptoms, TMDs can be divided into separate diagnostic subgroups based on their etiopathogenesis and/or pathophysiology. The diagnostic subgroups are characterized by a morphofunctional origin of the signs and symptoms, their localization and the pathophysiological process of origin [3, 4, 9, 16]:

- myofascial pain involves pathophysiological changes in muscles and/or tendons;
- anterior disc displacement or internal derangement implies changes in the structure or position of the disc with respect to the condyle, the most important being an intra-articular disorder.
- osteoarthritis of the temporomandibular joint includes localized active and inactive degenerative changes of cartilaginous articular planes and osseous structures.

The greatest prevalence of TMDs is in the adult female population aged between 18 and 45 [17]. Degenerative changes in the joints are generally more common in an older population, which does not mean that osteoarthritis does not also affect a younger population.

PAIN MEDICINE

The biomedical approach to TMDs diagnostics and treatment attaches considerable importance to the development of chronic pain, which is a common characteristic of other musculoskeletal disorders in the body. Thus, a recent common opinion is that TMDs are of unknown, idiopathic origin and the correlation between certain etiological factors cannot be fully confirmed, whereas the issue of chronic musculoskeletal (or nonmalignant) pain becomes dominant within the specialist field of pain medicine [18].

The application of etiopathogenetic models of the origin of TMDs (biopsychosocial and multifactorial concepts) in certain patients with clinical signs and symptoms is not entirely possible and therefore, the application of personalized/person-centered medicine concepts in chronic pain management is necessary [19]. Orofacial pain (musculoskeletal, neuropathic, neurovascular) has a prevalence of up to between 22% and 26% in the general population, of whom between 7% and 11% experience chronic pain [14, 20]. The prevalence of pain in the TMJ and masticatory muscles is relatively low (between 2% to 7%). Emergency cases in oral surgery are mostly consequences of odontogenic complications and soft tissue injuries (33.94% and 22.54% respectively), whereas TMJ disorders and trigeminal neuralgia account for less than 2% (1.63% and 1.34% respectively) [21, 22]. Chronic pain has a multidimensional character and is not determined solely by the period of duration (in general in excess of six months). It is non-somatic in origin and long-term peripheral sensitization increases pain in the nociceptors as a consequence, which leads to functional, neuroplastic changes in the central nervous system. The complexity of chronic pain is affected by psychological factors that play an important role in the complicated interaction of neurophysical, psychological and sociocultural factors [23]. Although the psychological factor is pronounced in the process of temporomandibular pain chronification, TMDs are not psychological or social disorders. Rollman et al. [24] did not find any significance either in the influence of depression, somatization and anxiety, or that of a number of social factors (employment, and household situation), on the improvement of TMD-pain complaints, and in the six-month follow-up study there was no controlled type of treatment or implementation of that treatment. In cases of chronic pain with a lack of nociceptive information, the patient still feels persistent pain, which is termed secondary hyperalgesia. This form of neural plasticity occurs due to genetic and environmental factors relating to the patient and they lead to central sensitization, which another form results in allodynia. Unexpected painful clinical conditions can be explained in this way, whereby the low threshold sensory inputs via central sensitization of the somato-sensory pathways may lead to a feeling of pain through activated synaptic connections. Pain became 'centralized' instead of being exclusively peripherally driven: there is an uncoupling of the clear stimulus response relationship that defines nociceptive pain. Painful TMDs have a pathophysiological basis in the specific genotype and phenotype of the patient which affects the manifestation of pain explained by the model of central sensitization [25].

PSYCHOLOGICAL CONTRIBUTION

Patients with chronic musculoskeletal pain often demonstrate a disproportion between relatively poorly present pathology and very strongly expressed symptoms of TMDs. Pain diagnostics and the evaluation of its somatic substrate is important for planning treatment in TMDs of myogenic and/or arthrogenic origin [26].

In 1959 Laszlo L. Schwartz developed an etiological model that stresses the psychosomatic constitutional factor in the development of TMDs, terming it TMJJ pain-dysfunction syndrome. He did not consider that the determined occlusal disorder was the cause but thought that in most cases it was the consequence of TMD signs and symptoms [26].

Psychological factors can be a part of the predisposition toward TMDs and the psycho-social ones are considered to be perpetual factors (social, behavioral and emotional difficulties). These factors affect the possibility of functional adaptation because their participation in creating emotional states and personal characteristics lowers the adaptational capacity of the masticatory system. Such psychological factors can be behavioral, cognitive and affective.

A behavioral factor involves oral appearance, problems with muscular tension, reaction to pain and to lifestyle-related activities. The cognitive category includes thoughts, beliefs and observations, that is, the contraproductive process of the ability to think. The affective one implies prolonged negative emotions, which include anxiety, depression, aggression, frustration and similar states [11, 27].

Stress is a condition where here is negative strain on the organism caused by various somatic and/or psychological stimuli and noxes (stressors). The patient's personality structure is related to the stress reaction conditioned by painful muscular hyperactivity. Expressing emotional opinions is subject to strong social control as it is often suppressed by emotions, which can lead to chronic muscular tension.

Taking note of stressful situations and coping with them is learned behaviour. Different situations may cause muscular tension because they are a form of strain, and empirical studies show a connection between different levels of stress indicators and temporomandibular disorders. Although there is no significant connection, the reduction of stress has an effect on the outcome of the treatment of dysfunction [28]. Epidemiological data show a relationship between muscular symptoms and emotional strain, but not in the case of arthrogenic symptoms [29].

The most important psychological factors pertaining to TMDs are anxiety and depression [11]. Patients with TMDs are significantly more depressed and anxious than other groups of dental patients and healthy asymptomatic subjects [30]. The prevalence of anxiety in TMDs ranges from 17% to 26% of patients and that of depression from 18% to 38% [31].

Somatization implies behavior in which psychological conflicts are transferred to physical ailments and thus an unloading is achieved. The patients avoid interpreting their 'actual problems' by developing ailments and complaining about pain, primarily in the stomach and mouth, and also in the form of headaches. Somatization was determined in about one quarter of patients with TMDs [32, 33].

Psychosocial factors are relevant to the transformation of acute temporomandibular into chronic pain, but it is difficult to determine an actual relationship between certain factors. In 20% to 40% of patients, chronic pain can be conditioned by severe psychosocial disturbances [34]. The high intensity of chronic temporomandibular pain and increased somatization are related to pain in the intraoral and extraoral muscles [35]. Anxiety as a potential etiological factor changes oral habits and increases muscular tension, and it can also alter the patient's perception of pain, depression too.

Because of the variable relationship between the patient's clinical signs and subjective symptoms, psychometric measuring is included in TMD diagnostics and it diagnoses the psychological/psychosocial status of the patient. Psychological evolution of the condition of the patient and the latter's reactions to clinical condition are most pronounced in cases of chronic pain in the masticatory system [36].

The RDC/TMD Axis II [15] does not include anxiety measuring, but Spielberger's STAI [37] is one easy-to-use instrument in practice as well as a screening measure. STAI (Y-form) in the form of a self-questionnaire determines anxiety as a current state (STAI 1) and as a general characteristic of a person (anxiety as a general state in the past period, STAI 2) by exceeding test-standardized marginal values.

Research Report

Our open prospective study conducted between 2001 and 2012, included patients with TMJ disorder (TMJD), of which 144 (mean age 32.47 years) had a primary diagnosis of disc displacement and 93 (mean age 48.82 years) one of osteoarthritis. A disproportion in the distribution of patients according to age groups is best illustrated by a partially age-related occurrence of TMJDs diagnoses, which predominate in females (Figure 1).

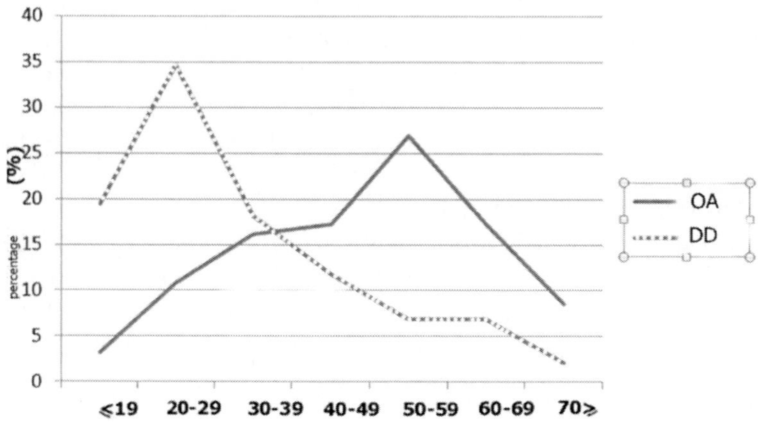

Figure 1. Comparison of the percentage of age prevalence in patients with disc displacement (DD), and osteoarthritis (OA) of temporomandibular joint.

Material and Methods

Inclusion Diagnostic Criteria

All the participants of both groups consisted of consecutively examined patients with internal derangement of the TMJ who were referred to the Department of Removable Prosthodontics at the School of Dental Medicine. The inclusion criteria for 'disc displacement' were pain and clicking or a history of clicking and limited mouth opening. The inclusion criteria for 'osteoarthritis' were pain and crepitation with or without limited mouth opening. Clinical diagnosis was verified on the basis of a history of TMD, clinical diagnostics according to Research Diagnostic Criteria (RDC)/TMD Axis I, and further refined diagnostics were provided by a manual functional analysis according to Bumann and Groot Landeweer [15, 38]. The definitive diagnosis and selection of the appropriate diagnostic subgroup were undertaken according to the MRI findings, where the primary diagnosis of disc displacement did not include clinical signs or radiological symptoms of osteoarthritis, whereas in the subgroup of patients with a primary diagnosis of osteoarthritis there was possible comorbidity with disc displacement.

Clinical signs and painful symptoms as well as crepitation in the TMJ were criteria for the diagnosis of osteoarthritis, regardless of comorbidity with disc displacement. The presence of pain in the joint alone, with osteoarthritic changes of the joint and physiological disc position visible on MRI were also criteria for a primary diagnosis of osteoarthritis. Previous pain duration suffered by the patients prior to the first examination was recorded as well as pain intensity on a visual-analogue scale (0, painless condition; 10, the strongest pain ever experienced) in an open mouth position [39]. Prior to this investigation, all participants had signed an informed consent form, and the investigation of this chapter was approved by the Ethics Committee of the School of Dental Medicine at the University of Zagreb, Croatia.

MRI Protocol

The bilateral MRI of the TMJ was performed with the following spin-echo-sequent parameters using a 1 T scanner Magnetom Harmony (Siemens, Erlangen, Germany): T_1 weighted image TR/TE 450/12, T_2 weighted image TR 3000/TE 66, field of view of 160 x 160, matrix of 256 x 192 and 3 mm slice), and using a 1.5T scanner Magnetom Avanto (Siemens, Erlangen, Germany) T_1 weighted image TR/TE 410/9.4, T_2 weighted image TR 460/TE 15, field of view of 180 x 180, matrix of 410 x 512 and 2 mm slice). All subjects were scanned in both the closed and open mouth positions. The angle of the parasagittal imaging is individually determined by that shown on the individual angulated layers of the axial and coronal slices.

The physiological position of the disc was defined according to the placement of its inter-medial zone between the articular eminence and the shortest distance of the bone contours of the ventrocranial part of the condyles in the parasagittal plane in the closed mouth position [40].

The following cortical bone and disc morphology abnormalities were analysed on the TMJ examined, i.e., the configuration and contours of the articular eminence (normal shape or bone sclerosis with loss of shape) and condylar head (normal shape, deplaned shape, and osteoarthritic changes, such as sclerosed areas, and with osteophytes).

Anxiety Measuring

The psychological assessment was carried out using Spielberger's State-Trait Anxiety Inventory (STAI) Form Y [37]. STAI is the definitive instrument for measuring anxiety and contains four-point Likert items for self-report measure. Scores range from twenty to eighty, the higher the score, the greater the anxiety. The STAI 1 test measures anxiety as a subjective state, a feeling lasting for a week, including the day of testing, and STAI test 2 measures anxiety as a relatively stable individual characteristic throughout life in general.

Statistical Analysis

Statistical data analysis was performed using the STATISTICA (StatSoft Inc., Tulsa, Oklahoma, USA) program, while differences in distribution were analysed through Pearson correlation analysis.

Results

Table 1 shows the basic values tested for the subgroup of patients with disc displacement. The correlation analysis (Table 2) revealed a positive correlation between the patient's age and higher anxiety on both STAI scales and also on VAS. In addition, present anxiety (STAI 1 scores) is higher in patients with general anxiety (STAI 2 scores) and those who experienced greater pain intensity on VAS. Pain duration prior to the first examination did not correlate significantly with any other variables.

Table 1. Basic values of the tested variables of patients with disc displacement

Variables	mean	SD	minimum value	maximum value
pain duration (in months)	14.25	21.18	0.20	101.00
STAI 1 scores	38.26	9.87	20.00	72.00
STAI 2 scores	39.72	8.31	24.00	65.00
pain on VAS	6.02	1.76	2.00	10.00

SD, standard deviation; STAI, State-Trait Anxiety Inventory; VAS, visual-analogue scale.

Table 2. Correlation analysis of variables of patients with disc displacement (*marked Pearson Correlation Coefficients are significant at $p<0.05$)

variables	pain duration	STAI 1	STAI 2	pain on VAS
Age	0.054085	0.187248*	0.295994*	0.189169*
pain duration		-0.004510	0.066254	0.045809
STAI 1			0.690661*	0.217118*
STAI 2				0.109680

STAI, State-Trait Anxiety Inventory; VAS, visual-analogue scale.

Table 3 shows the basic values of the variables for the subgroup of patients with a primary diagnosis of osteoarthritis. Compared with patients with a primary diagnosis of disc displacement, measured anxiety showed higher average values.

Table 3. Basic values of tested variables of patients with osteoarthritis

variables	mean	SD	minimum value	maximum value
Pain duration (in months)	14.24	18.35	0.50	120.00
STAI 1 scores	41.00	9.60	20.00	64.00
STAI 2 scores	42.99	9.32	23.00	73.00
Pain on VAS	6.38	1.54	3.00	9.50

SD, standard deviation; STAI, State-Trait Anxiety Inventory; VAS, visual-analogue scale.

There was no higher prevalence of a statistically significant correlation of variables in patients with osteoarthritis (Table 4) compared with those with disc displacement (Table 2). The osteoarthritic patients were elderly, and showed higher anxiety scores on both STAI scales, and the only significant correlation was determined for the patients' age and current anxiety levels (STAI 1), while there was no significant co-dependence between the two qualitative anxiety measures (STAI 1 and STAI 2).

Table 4. Correlation analysis of variables of patients with osteoarthritis (*marked Pearson Correlation Coefficients are significant at $p<0.05$)

variables	pain duration	STAI 1	STAI 2	pain on VAS
age	-0.17137	0.21059*	0.19465	0.09595
pain duration		0.07267	0.17825	-0.20380
STAI 1			0.69194*	0.14852
STAI 2				0.15393

STAI, State-Trait Anxiety Inventory; VAS, visual-analogue scale.

Clinical Reports

Anamnestic data and also medical documentation of all patients were collected for the study and analysed as a part of the multidisciplinary management of each patient. Certain patients had a previous medical history of psychological and/or psychiatric treatment. Certain clinical cases are described as a part of a long-term follow-up of patients.

Case 1

The case presented is that of a 36-year-old female patient, who was referred to the School of Dental Medicine, in 2008, on the recommendation of a friend, due to discomfort in the left TMJ. She first experienced stiffness of the jaw when opening her mouth fifteen years earlier and this was accompanied by severe pain, which would subside after ten to fifteen minutes. Episodes of stiffness and pain continued to occur occasionally.

In 2002, she visited a specialist in oral surgery and prosthodontics and then obtained an upper occlusal splint, which she wore only one month due to a traffic accident and her husband's health problems. When she tried to wear the splint again after some time, it was no longer adapted to her upper dental arch. Since then, she suffered from the aforementioned problems, but she did not seek treatment. With regard to bruxism, the patient herself noticed nocturnal teeth clenching during the night, and frequent nocturnal spasms of the masticatory muscles.

Clinical Examination and Diagnosis

Manual functional analysis in 2008 revealed crepitus with pain in the left joint (diagnosis of osteoarthritis) and pain with limited opening in the right TMJ. A classification system using RDC/TMD in the left TMJ showed a diagnosis of osteoarthritis (group III) [15, 38].

During passive compression (bilaminar zone), none of the TMJs showed provoked pain, and therefore, the diagnosis of anterior disc displacement without reduction by manual functional analysis in right TMJ could not be determined with certainty [38].

The visual analogue scale (VAS: 0, no pain; 10 most severe pain) measured the intensity of pain in the left TMJ: active opening range was 42 mm and the pain was VAS = 5.5. Pain on palpation of the left TMJ was VAS = 7.5, while the patient felt minimal pain at rest, VAS = 1.5. Passive opening capacity also accompanied by pain in the left TMJ was 50 mm. In addition, a right laterotrusive movement caused pain in the left TMJ, although the left (9.5 mm) and right (10 mm) laterotrusion were quite symmetrical.

Radiological Diagnostics

MRI showed anterior disc displacement without reduction in the left TMJ with expressed degenerative changes (Figure 2), while the right TMJ showed anterior disc displacement with reduction (Figure 3). Computerized tomography (CT) showed marked osteoarthritic changes on the left condyle; anteriorly located osteophytes with subchondral degenerative changes of the condyle and narrowed joint space of the left TMJ (Figure 4).

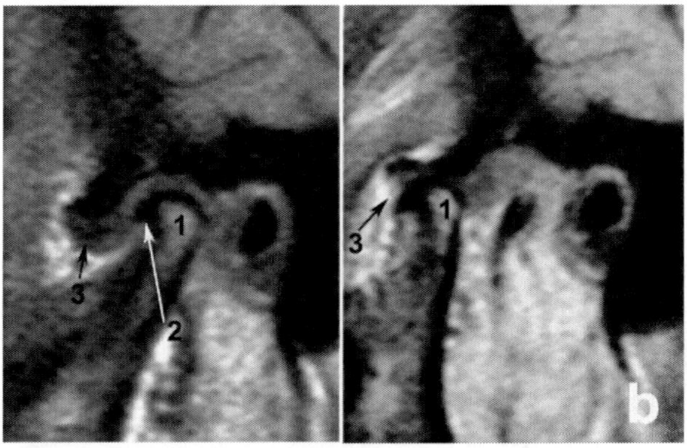

Figure 2. Magnetic resonance imaging of the anteriorly displaced disc with osteoarthritis of the left temporomandibular joint in the sagittal plane (a; 1 condyle; 2 osteophyte; 3 DD without reduction; left – closed mouth, right – open mouth).

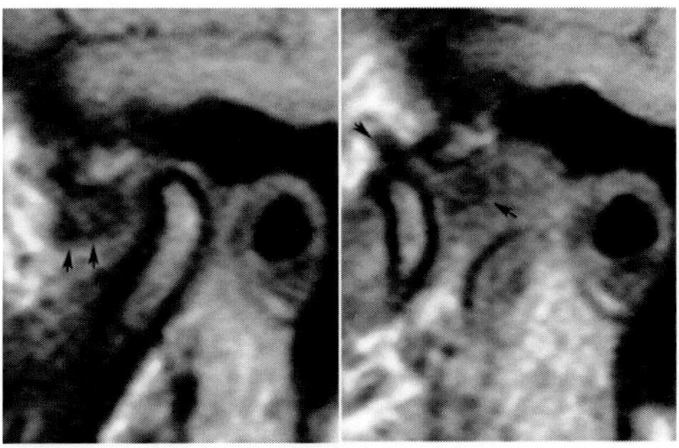

Figure 3. Magnetic resonance imaging of the right temporomandibular joint in closed mouth (left) and open mouth (right) positions (arrow – DD with reduction).

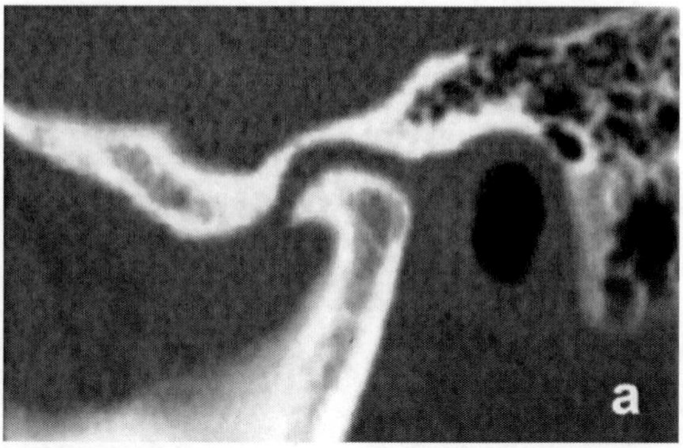

Figure 4. Computerized tomography of the left temporomandibular joint.

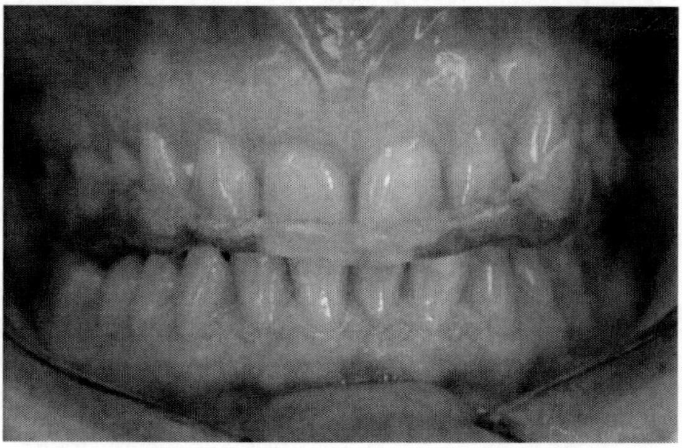

Figure 5. Michigan splint on the upper dental arch.

Mental Health

The patient informed us about her bipolar disorder, as well as about her numerous symptoms and their repercussions of her social, intimate and working environments. Unrecognized and untreated postpartum depression represented, in the patient's retrospective opinion, the first sign of compromised mental health. She occasionally resorted to therapy (multiple medications in different periods of the recent past from the group of selective serotonin reuptake inhibitors). The patient did not bring accompanying medical records, but a high level of anxiety was registered using STAI (Y-form) [30]. The patient revealed the following values: STAI 1=42 and STAI 2=46 (marginal values by age and sex for STAI 1 = 36.17 and STAI 2 = 36.15).

Occlusal Splint

Although the stabilization splint is recommended for patients with osteoarthritis since it is similar to the morphology of occlusal surfaces of the dental arch on which it is located (usually the upper dental arch), the upper Michigan splint made from light-curing acrylics was fabricated for the patient on account of her bruxism (Figure 5). The Michigan splint has a distinctive almost flat occlusal surface, which, besides programming the masticatory muscles and positioning the condyles in relation to the anterior position of the disc and the entire glenoid fossa, also enables smooth performance of bruxism movements [41]. The relatively flat surfaces of the occlusal splint, which are in contact with working cusps of opposing (mandibular) teeth, enable smooth adjustment of the position of the mandible within 'freedom in centric', and also protect hard dental tissues against bruxist movements. Increasing the vertical dimension for the amount of the interocclusal free space also affects masticatory muscle relaxation.

Three-Year Follow-Up

The patient wore a Michigan splint, but not regularly, and after three years (2011), a new Michigan splint for the upper dental arch was fabricated. During the follow-up in 2011, active mouth opening was slightly larger (44 mm). Pain in the left TMJ was gone after only six months of therapy. Since then, there had been no pain in any of the joints, while in the left there was no crepitation. Pronounced clicking in the right TMJ during the final stage of mouth opening occurred five to six months after the first examination, diagnosis, and wearing of splint. The current level of anxiety (follow-up in 2011), using STAI 1 was 56, which shows an obvious increase.

Case 2

A female 32-year-old patient came to the clinic due to pain in the left temporomandibular joint which had started two years before (October 2011). In the previous period she underwent extensive medical and oral-surgical treatments but without success or being given a definitive diagnosis of TMJ disorder. Prior to the occurrence of the painful symptomatology she had experienced painless clicking on maximum mouth opening in the same joint. On one occasion she woke up feeling a short-term probing pain, swelling of the left TMJ and limited mouth opening. At the same time she felt pain below the left edge of the mandibular corpus, but this pain was unrelated to mouth opening.

Medical Diagnostics and Maxilofacial Surgical Examination

At first, she was admitted in November 2011 to the infectology department of the clinical hospital where she underwent testing for five days due to TMJ symptoms. Prior to hospitalization she had received antibiotics (clindamycin) intravenously and she was afebrile the entire time. Since there was no improvement, a maxillofacial surgeon was consulted during her hospital treatment. An inflammation of the parotid gland was determined by ultrasound, with undeniable clinical symptoms of TMJ disorder. The maxillofacial surgeon concluded that it was a case of first stage trismus of the masseter muscle, which would explain limited mouth opening. Further examinations focused on the parotid inflammation and the patient was referred for a second opinion to the clinical hospital, also to a maxillofacial surgeon, who treated her from January till March 2012. Further examinations were complemented by CT diagnostics (Figure 6) which excluded parotid pathology.

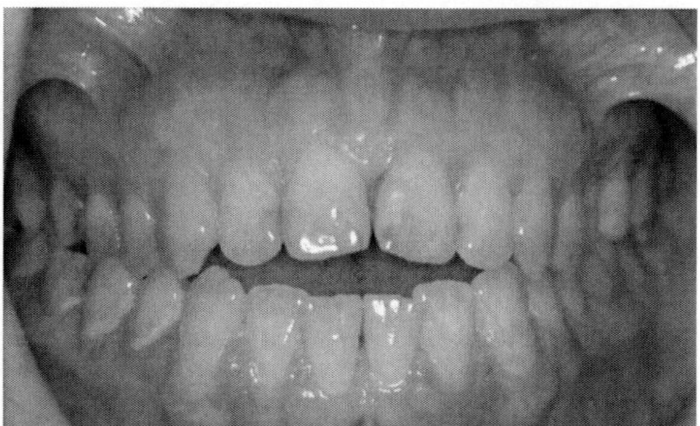

Figure 6. Habitual occlusion of the female patient (note open anterior bite).

Only the indications of articular planes' sclerosation were determined along the elongated styloid processes without any manifested symptomatology of Eagle's syndrome (pain along the lower mandibular edge does not increase with swallowing).

In the same clinical hospital, the patient was instructed in oral exercises and because of a pronounced finding of open bite and diagnosed nocturnal bruxism, she was given an occlusal splint. She had to travel 400 km in one direction to have the splint fabricated. However, she had worn the splint on her upper jaw only fifteen days when it broke along the medial line. She had it repaired but it continued to break and she had noticed nocturnal teeth grinding.

Neurological Examination

In December 2012 she visited the neurologist who focused on the typical neurological parameters in the findings, i.e., no facial or trigeminal asymmetry, no lateralization or motor asymmetry, regular coordination and target movements and also regular, reflexes. The neurologist suggested psychological testing of the patient.

Psychological Examination

Here current intellectual achievement was evaluated as high average. The analysis showed fatigue with concentration disturbances. There were no significant oscillations in the examined memory modalities. She had above average results on the visual-perceptive organization test and the visual-motor coordination test. The emotional profile revealed extraversion, sociability with traits of social caution and responsibility, with a preference for retreating and passivity during frustration. She showed latent anxiety with a tendency toward negation in emotional issues. The results of cognitive function tests did not show deficits of an organicity type, whereas the emotional status showed a latent anxious component in a controlled personality.

Clinical Examination and Radiological Diagnosis

In October 2013, the patient was referred by her dentist to the School of Dental Medicine, Department of Removable Prosthodontics where thorough clinical and MRI diagnostics were performed. A clinical examination determined arthralgia of the left TMJ as well as pain on palpation during dynamic compressions and translations. A painful subluxation setting of the condyle occurred during maximum mouth opening as well as light clicking on medial translation in the left TMJ. Isometric strain was felt in the masseter on the left. Pain on opening was on VAS 7.8, on palpation 7.5 and in the resting position 5.2. Maximum mouth opening was 49 mm. Deflexion in the middle of the mandible was on the painful left side on mouth opening. Clinically, this was determined as tendomyopathy of the masseter and partial anterior displacement of the left TMJ with repositioning, according to Bumann and Groot Landeweer. Magnetic resonance confirmed the symptomatology of the left TMJ, while MRI showed partial anterior disc displacement without reduction and without degenerative changes (Figure 7).

Psychological testing according to Spielberger's STAI showed scores below the limit for present anxiety (on STAI 1=32; marginal value by age and sex for STAI 1 is 36.17), and mildly elevated scores on STAI 2=38 for anxiety in general (marginal value by age and sex for STAI 2 is 36.15).

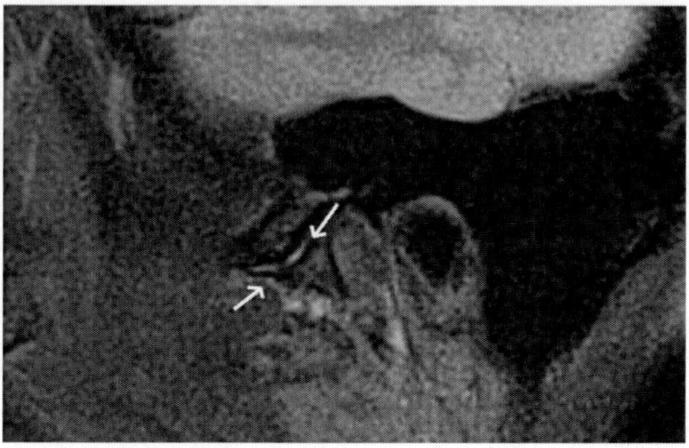

Figure 7. Disc displacement in the left temporomandibular joint (arrows shows displaced disc).

Since there was a gap of three months between the first examination and MRI recording and because of the distance involved and work obligations, she did not begin any therapy. In the aforementioned time period the patient experienced mutable pain with periods of remission and even without any treatment, a painless state was achieved with discomfort in the symptomatic joint. However, she was still interested in getting treatment and in collaboration with a physiatrist-rheumatologist (along with a diagnosed cervicocranial syndrome), physical therapy of the TMJ and the cervical spine was arranged in her home town.

Case 3

In December 2008, a retired fifty-four-year-old female patient was referred to the School of Dental Medicine because of pain in the left TMJ. She had experienced pain there on mouth opening and chewing since 2006 and since August 2008 and also clicking. She had difficulty locating the exact site of the pain, but she felt it deep in the preauricular region and along the mandibular ramus. The pain was felt only during mandibular movements and it increased on mouth opening. She had previously seen an otorhinolaryngologist and had an x-ray of the left TMJ on which a shallow furrow was visible on the compact of the condylar head, while joint mobility in an open mouth position was rated as normal. Although the otorhinolaryngologist made a diagnosis of arthritis of the TMJ, he also recommended cold compresses along with nonsteroidal antirheumatics as well as a softer diet and antibiotics.

Clinical Examination and Radiological Diagnosis

Clinical examination confirmed the clinical signs and symptoms of osteoarthritis of the left TMJ: on active movements there were crepitations in the joint as well as on dynamic compressions and translations, whereas the same joint was more painful on passive compressions which pointed to an anteriorly displaced disc. She rated the pain on mandibular movements 7.5 on VAS. Mouth opening amounted to 40.5 mm.

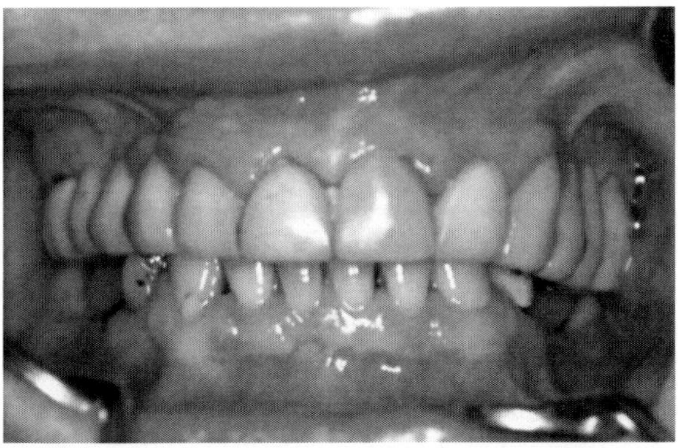

Figure 8. Habitual occlusion of the female patient.

The patient did not wear a partial lower prosthetic appliance and there were no occlusal contacts in the abutment regions (Figure 8). She stated that since she had obtained the prosthetic appliance four years ago, she had a high bite on the left side and due to this she had never even worn it. Subjectively, she did not relate the symptoms of the left TMJ to the unsuccessful prosthetic treatment.

MRI confirmed the clinical diagnostics: pronounced osteoarthritic changes of the entire condylar head with mildly pronounced, anterior osteophyte and deplaned articulation plane. The disc was displaced without reduction, but quite shattered in shape (Figure 9). The inflammatory exudate in the articular space is better visible in open mouth position.

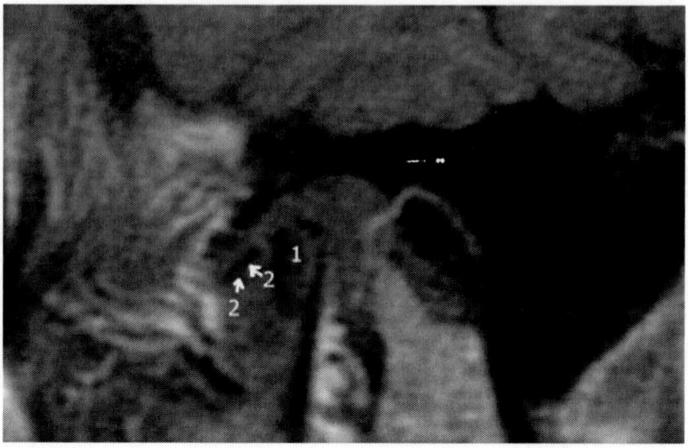

Figure 9. Magnetic resonance imaging of the anteriorly displaced disc with osteoarthritis of the left temporomandibular joint in the sagittal plane (1, condyle; 2, disc).

Noting the Psychological State

Although during the first examination the patient did not show any signs of psychological nature, at the second examination she explained what was bothering her. When an MRI was suggested, she consulted her general practitioner who made a comment about her 'going under radiation again' which implied a previous x-ray of the spine. Although the physical effects of the MRI on the body need not be explained here, she put this into the context of another of her illnesses, i.e., panic disorder. After a month, the patient voluntarily accepted MRI diagnostics. Although she never submitted any medical records, she described her mental issues. She had worked as a nurse in a hospital and once pricked herself with a needle, and although there was never any infection, she started to suffer from chronic fear. She also stated that twelve years before she started suffering from postpartum depression. She could not control her fears about the sterility of objects and being pricked as well as becoming infected and she had to be retired. She described in detail the impact of these fears on her everyday life. She did not leave the house due to her phobias, she was afraid of giving blood samples in laboratories (fear of AIDS, hepatitis B and C), at home she often wiped the surfaces which she used with alcohol and vinegar. Once she mentioned seeing blood on the pavement when she was with her grandchildren and although she knew the children did not touch it, she experienced multiple fears of infection due to the incident. When going to the market, if she heard sirens, she assumed her apartment was on fire, which resulted in panic attacks.

Her statements proved helpful during her examination in the dental chair because she admitted having fears about the sterility of the dental unit and that the instruments (dental mirror, probe, etc.) might become infected (from falling onto the floor, etc.).

Psychological testing according to Spielberger's STAI showed a high level of anxiety which confirmed the patient's history. Scores on STAI 1 were 51 with marginal value by age and sex 32.20 and scores on STAI 2 were 66 with marginal value by age and sex 31.79.

During the initial examination and while waiting for MRI findings, the patient stated that the painful symptoms in the left TMJ had disappeared and only crepitations were clinically present. She continued the treatment for panic disorder in the form of group psychotherapy and medication (the tricyclic antidepressant clomipramine). The painless crepitations did not require any planning of initial treatment because they did not disturb the TMJ function.

Follow-Up during 5-Year-Period

During the entire period of the follow-up there was no remission of the painful symptoms of TMJ disorder. There were still crepitations in the left TMJ. Mouth opening amounted to 45.5 mm. Although the patient still suffered from panic disorder, she regularly went to group therapy and claimed her psychological state had improved in comparison with previous years.

DISCUSSION

As in many other musculoskeletal disorders of the human body, the modern biomedical viewpoint is that they are of nonspecific etiopathology, that is, idiopathic if seen at the level of the individual patient [8]. Correlating TMDs with numerous etiopathogenic factors does not lead to an effective understanding of their causal relationship. The biopsychosocial conceptualization of the pain experience recognized psychological factors as a part of multidimensional description of pain, especially chronically painful conditions such as TMJD [19].

The prevalence of chronic pain according to the World Health Organization averages 22%, and almost 50% of chronic pain is due to musculoskeletal pain [42]. There is a lack of absolute criteria for identifying the presence of central sensitization (reversible increase in the excitability and synaptic efficacy of neurons in central nociceptive pathways caused by nociceptive input trigger), which includes numerous clinical syndromes. Degenerative joint disease (osteoarthritis) has the greatest impact on health in the general population, and particularly the TMDs, which is related to the topic of this chapter. At the same time, other oral conditions as a consequence of surgical procedures can cause central sensitization, for example, third molar extraction [25].

With increasing age, the prevalence of TMD symptoms decreases but there is a slightly higher prevalence of clinical signs. The greatest prevalence is in women of reproductive age. This shows that various forms of TMDs generally do not progress, depending on increasing age [4, 5, 14, 17]. The age difference in patients with various TMJ diagnoses was noticed with regard to the diagnosis of disc displacement and osteoarthritis. Similar results were shown in our study sample. The gender prevalence of females is not only explained by social factors but also by genetics. Potential hormonal mediation should also be taken into consideration since the prevalence decreases in postmenopausal age [43].

In clinical symptomatology which involves sounds in the TMJ (clicking, crepitation) and reduced mouth opening, the symptom of arthralgia (joint pain) is the most common symptom that causes patients to seek diagnosis and treatment. Benoliel & Sharav [14] reported that clinical forms of orofacial pains are well defined but that there is a possibility of them being unrecognized, that is, confused with musculoskeletal pain and neuropathic orofacial pain (trigeminal neuralgia, particularly unusual trigeminal neuralgia presentation) [44].

The psychological factors play an important role in the expression of pain during different stages of TMD, especially in perpetuation of TMD and in the response of such patients to treatment. There is no clear distinction between acute and chronic pain, and there is also no clearly defined role of psychological factors in the course of treatment. Higher level of anxiety in TMD patients can be a risk for chronic pain development and bruxism [45]. However, contrary to the relationship between chronic pain and anxiety, Giannankopoulos et al. [46] found the importance of depression for women with chronic pain, from a muscular diagnosis according to Research Diagnostic Criteria (RDC)/TMD Axis I [17]. According to Akar et al. [47], a higher degree of depression was found in patients with TMJ disorder and higher somatization in patients with pain that were referred. Chronic pain had an impact on the patients with TMDs, where severe or moderate somatization and depression were determined (scores from 47.7% to 1.8% depending on psychological disorder and the psychological instrument used) [48].

Pain related to TMDs is mostly the consequence of peripheral nociceptive activity [19]. Gustin et al. [49] did not prove changes in the mass of grey matter in TMD patients compared with neuropathic pain patients who had decreased thalamic volume and neural viability. Compared with results by Younger et al. [50], who determined that TMD pain is associated with thalamic grey matter volume increases, this can be explained by the influence on thalamic anatomy, of the affective state in TMD patients.

Psychological factors can be used to explain why some patients are disturbed by their symptoms and why only a small proportion of patients with the symptoms (around 5%) seek treatment. Certain insights help us to determine the patients' reactions to a symptom and decide on the right treatment. The patients' need for treatment is explained by these factors, and when a patient considers the pain to be life threatening, then he or she shows elevated anxiety and seeks medical help [5, 51].

There are diseases of oral mucosa, the occurrence of which is closely related to anxiety. Oral lichen planus is a T-cell mediated disease to a still unknown antigen, closely related to stress and psychological disturbances. According to Valter et al. [52], in a group of such patients STAI 1 amounted to 44.76 on average, and STAI 2 45.16, which are values higher than in a recent study with patients diagnosed with TMJ disorder.

In the general population (mean age 42.1 years) with a depressive and/or anxiety disorder who were followed for two years, Gerrits et al. [28] found that the most frequent pain location was the head (76.6%), and on the contrary, the least frequent was orofacial pain (18.1%). Joint pain was reported by 51.9% of the subjects, and it was only significant in the presence of a depressive and/or anxiety disorder.

Reversible, non-invasive therapeutic means are recommended for the treatment. Dentists most often use the Michigan splint. Other frequently used options for the treatment of temporomandibular pain require a multidisciplinary approach, i.e., physical therapy and kinesiotherapy, acupuncture, non-steroidal anti-inflammatory drugs, biofeedback and psychotherapy [53, 54].

The gold standard for diagnosing a TMJ disorder as well as for the use of radiological diagnostics of soft intraarticular tissue is magnetic resonance imaging (MRI). Apart from the nonspecific presentation of the TMJs on the panoramic radiograph, with respect to the clinical diagnosis of osteoarthritis, radiological diagnostics included highly specific methods for detection of hard tissue - CT [55].

Conclusion

Positive clinical findings of arthrogenic disorder indicated further radiological diagnostics, that is, magnetic resonance imaging and computed tomography. MRI serves as the gold standard in the diagnosis of disc displacement and also for displaying TMJ hard tissue.

Although there was a high average value of anxiety in a large group of patients with TMJ disorder, there was no single relation to previous TMJ pain duration. Chronic pain, as a multidimensional experience and as an illness with its own symptoms and complications, requires an individual approach, particularly in the evaluation of treatment success.

Anxiety was detected in certain patients from this study, which involves the doctor-patient relationship in adequate evaluation, assessment and monitoring of diagnostic and therapeutic modalities directed to the illness, while not neglecting pain and psychological status.

References

[1] Durham, J. (2008) Temporomandibular disorders (TMD): an overview. *Oral Surgery. 1*, 60-68.

[2] Hamdan, E., Bouzubar, F.F. & Landry, M.D. (2013). The Bone and Joint Decade (BJD) initiative: how did Kuwait perform? *Journal of World Health and Population. 14*, 5-11.

[3] Learreta, J.A., Matos, J.L., Matos, M.F. & Durst, A.C. (2009). Current diagnosis of temporomandibular pathologies. *Cranio: the Journal of Craniomandibular Practice. 27*, 125-133.

[4] Palla, S. (2003). Myoarthropatischer Schmerz: oft verkannt. *Schmerz. 17*, 425-431.

[5] Badel, T. *Temporomandibularni poremećaji i stomatološka protetika.* Zagreb: Medicinska naklada; 2007.

[6] Carlsson, G.E. (2010). Some dogmas related to prosthodontics, temporomandibular disorders and occlusion. *Acta Odontologica Scandinavica, 68*, 313-322.

[7] Oakley, M. & Vieira, A.R. (2008). The many faces of the genetics contribution to temporomandibular joint disorder. *Orthodontics & Craniofacial Research, 11*, 125-135.

[8] Green, S.C. Concepts of TMD Etiology: Effects on Diagnosis and Treatment, In: Laskin, D.M.; Green, C.S. & Hylander, W.L., editors. *TMDs. An Evidence-Based Approach to Diagnosis and Treatment*, Chicago: Quintessence; 2006; 219-228.

[9] Emshoff, R., Innerhofer, K., Rudisch, A. & Bertram, S. (2002). The biological concept of "internal derangement and osteoarthrosis": A diagnostic approach in patients with temporomandibular joint pain? *Oral surgery, oral medicine, oral pathology, oral radiology, and endodontics, 93*, 39-44.

[10] Türp JC. (2000). *Temporomandibular Pain - Clinical Presentation and Impact*. Berlin: Quintessenz-Verlag; 2000.

[11] De Boever, J.A. & Carlsson, G.E. Etiology and Differential Diagnosis. In: Zarb, G.A., Carlsson, G.E., Sessle, B.J. & Mohl, N.D., editors. *Temporomandibular Joint and Masticatory Muscle Disorders*. Copenhagen: Munksgaard; 1994; 171-187.

[12] Jürgens, J. (2009). Sechs Leitsymptome der Kiefergelenkarthropathie. *Deutsche Zahnärztliche Zeitschrift, 64*, 308-317.

[13] Badel, T., Savić Pavičin, I., Podoreški, D., Marotti, M., Krolo, I. & Grbeša, Đ. (2011). Temporomandibular joint development and functional disorders related to clinical otologic symptomatology. *Acta Clinica Croatica, 50*, 51-60.

[14] Benoliel, R. & Sharav, Y. (2010). Chronic orofacial pain. *Current pain and headache reports, 14*, 33-40.

[15] Dworkin, S.F. & LeResche, L. (1992). Research diagnostic criteria for temporomandibular disorders: Review, criteria, examinations and specifications, critique. *Journal of craniomandibular disorders : facial & oral pain, 6*, 301-355.

[16] Nassif, N.J. & Talic, Y.F. (2001). Classic symptoms in temporomandibular disorder patients: a comparative study. *Cranio: the Journal of Craniomandibular Practice, 19*, 33-41.

[17] de Bont, L.G., Dijkgraaf, L.C. & Stegenga, B. (1997). Epidemiology and natural progression of articular temporomandibular disorders. *Oral surgery, oral medicine, oral pathology, oral radiology, and endodontics*, 83, 72-76.

[18] Perosili-Gudelj, M. & Lončarić-Katušin, M. (2005). Chronic pain and its challenge facing the challenge of society on the threshold of the 3rd millenium. *Liječnički vjesnik, 127,* (Suppl), 107-109.

[19] Dougall, A.L., Jimenez, C.A., Haggard, R.A., Stowell, A.W., Riggs, R.R. & Gatchel, R.J. (2012). Biopsychosocial factors associated with the subcategories of acute temporomandibular joint disorders. *Journal of Orofacial Pain. 26*, 7-16.

[20] dos Santos Calderon P., Peixoto, R.F., Gomes, V.M., da Mota Corrêa, A.S., de Alencar, E.N, Rossetti, L.M. & Conti, P.C. (2012). Concordance among different pain scales in patients with dental pain. *Journal of Orofacial Pain, 26,* 126-131.

[21] Cooper, B,C. & Kleinberg, I. (2007). Examination of a large patient population for the presence of symptoms and signs of temporomandibular disorders. *Cranio: the Journal of Craniomandibular Practice, 25,* 114-126.

[22] Brajković, B. & Macan D. (2002). Analysis of Emergency Cases in the Clinic of Maxillofacial and Oral Surgery, Clinical Hospital"Dubrava". *Acta Stomatologica Croatica, 36*, 219-221.

[23] Schierz, O., Reiβmann, D.R. & Singer, S. (2013). Duration of pain as an indicator for psychosocial impairments in patients with temporomandibular disorders. *Journal of Craniomandibular Function, 5,* 229-245.

[24] Rollman, A., Visscher, C.M., Gorter, R.C. & Naeije, M. (2013). Improvement in patients with a TMD-pain report. A 6-month follow-up study. *Journal of Oral Rehabilitation, 40,* 5-14.

[25] Woolf, C.J. (2011) Central sensitization: Implication for the diagnosis and treatment of pain. *Pain, 152,* Suppl3, S2-15.

[26] Kanter, RJ. *Prevalence and etology of craniomandibular dysfunction: an epidemiological study of the Dutch adult.* Winssen: RP Scientifics; 1990.

[27] Arntz, A., Dreessen, L. & de Jong, P. (1994). The influence of anxiety on pain: attentional and attributional mediators. *Pain, 56*, 307-314.

[28] Gerrits, M.M., Vogelzangs, N., van Oppen, P., van Marwijk, H.W., van der Horst, H. & Penninx, B.W. (2012). Impact of pain on the course of depressive and anxiety disorders. *Pain, 153,* 429-436.

[29] Sieber, M., Grubenmann, E., Ruggia, G.M. & Palla, S. (2003). Relation between stress and symptoms of craniomandibular disorders in adolescents. *Schweizer Monatsschrift für Zahnmedizin, 113,* 648-654.

[30] Sirirungrojying, S., Srisintorn, S. & Akkayanont, P. (1998). Psychometric profiles of temporo-mandibular disorder patients in southern Thailand. *Journal of Oral Rehabilitation, 25*, 541-544.

[31] Yap, A.U.J., Chua, E.K. & Hoe, J.K.E. (2002). Clinical TMD, pain-related disability and psychological status of TMD patients. *Journal of Oral Rehabilitation, 29,* 374-380.

[32] Yap, A.U.J, Chua, E.K., Dworkin, S.F., Tan, H.H. & Tan, K.B.C. (2002). Multiple Pains and Psychological Functioning/Psychologic Distress in TMD Patients. *International Journal of Prosthodontics, 15*, 461-466.

[33] Ćelić, R., Braut, V. & Petričević N. (2011). Influence of depression and somatization on acute and chronic orofacial pain in patients with single or multiple TMD diagnoses. *Collegium Antropologicum, 35*, 709-713.

[34] Paak, S., Hugger, A., Bollmann, F. & Stüttgen U. (2001). Schmerzbezogene psychosoziale Aspekte bei Patienten der Myoarthropathie-Sprechstunde. *Deutsche Zahnärztliche Zeitschrift, 56,* 317-321.

[35] Wilson, L., Dworkin, S.F., Whitney, C. & LeResche, L. (1994). Somatization and pain dispersion in chronic temporomandibular disorder pain. *Pain, 57*, 55-61.

[36] Braš, M., Dorđević, V., Gregurek, R. & Bulajić M. (2010). Neurobiological and clinical relationship between psychiatric disorders and chronic pain. *Psychiatria Danubina, 22,* 221-226.

[37] Spielberger, C.D. *Priručnik za upitnik anksioznosti kao stanja i osobine ličnosti STAI.* Jastrebarsko: Slap; 2001.

[38] Bumann, A. & Lotzman, U. *TMJ Disorders and Orofacial Pain - The Role of Dentistry in a Multidisciplinary Diagnostic Approach.* Stuttgart: Thieme; 2002.

[39] Williamson, A. & Hoggart, B. (2005). Pain: a review of three commonly used pain rating scales. *Journal of Clinical Nursing, 14*, 798-804.

[40] Badel, T., Savić Pavičin, I., Jakovac, M., Kern, J. & Zadravec, D. (2013). Disc and Condylar Head Position in the Temporomandibular Joint With and Without Disc Displacement. *Collegium Antropologicum, 37*, 901-906.

[41] Badel, T., Simonić-Kocijan, S., Lajnert, V., Dulčić, N. &, Dijana Zadravec, D. (2013). Michigan splint and treatment of temporomandibular joint – review of literature. *Medicina Fluminensis, 49,* 112-120.

[42] Ćurković, B. (2005). Chronic musculoskeletal pain. *Liječnički vjesnik, 127*, Supl. 2, 111-114.

[43] Plesh, O., Noonan, C., Buchwald, D.S., Goldberg, J & Afari, N. (2012). Temporomandibular disorder-type pain and migraine headache in women: a preliminary twin study. *Journal of Orofacial Pain, 26,* 91-98.

[44] Badel, T., Savić Pavičin, I., Bašić Kes, V., Zavoreo, I., Zadravec, D. & Kern J. (2013). Orofacial pain caused by trigeminal neuralgia and/or temporomandibular disorders. *Periodicum Biologorum, 115*, 185-189.

[45] Badel, T., Keros, J., Marotti, M., Kern, J., Kocijan Lovko, S. & Rošin Grget, K. (2008). Therapy of displaced disk of the temporomandibular joint in relation to anxiety. *Periodicum Biologorum, 110,* 101-105.

[46] Giannakopoulos, N.N., Keller, L., Rammelsberg, P., Kronmüller, K.-T. & Schmitter, M. (2010) Anxiety and depression in patients with chronic temporomandibular pain and controls. *Journal of Dentistry, 38,* 369-376.

[47] Akar, G.C., Eryüksel, G. & Erdem, A. (2007). The Psychological Status in Patients with Temporomandibular Disorders in Turkish Population. *Acta Stomatologica Croatica, 41,* 345-354.

[48] Manfredini, D., Borella, L., Favero, L., Ferronato, G. & Guarda-Nardini, L. (2010). Chronic pain severity and depression/somatization levels in TMD patients. *International Journal of Prosthodontics, 23,* 529-34.

[49] Gustin, S.M., Peck, C.C., Wilcox, S.L., Nash, P.G., Murray, G.M. & Henderson, L.A. (2011). Different pain, different brain: thalamic anatomy in neuropathic and non-neuropathic chronic pain syndromes. *Journal of neuroscience: the official journal of the Society for Neuroscience, 31*, 5956-5964.

[50] Younger JW, Shen YF, Goddard G, Mackey SC. (2010). Chronic myofascial temporomandibular pain is associated with neural abnormalities in the trigeminal and limbic systems. *Pain, 149*, 222-228.

[51] Puretić, M.B & Demarin, V. (2012). Neuroplasticity mechanisms in the pathophysiology of chronic pain. *Acta Clinica Croatica, 51,* 425-429.

[52] Valter, K., Boras, V.V., Buljan, D., Juras, D.V., Sušić, M., Pandurić, D.G. & Verzak, Z. (2013). The influence of psychological state on oral lichen planus. *Acta Clinica Croatica, 52,* 145-149.

[53] Badel, T., Krapac, L. & Kraljević, A. (2012). The role of physical therapy in patients with temporomandibular joint disorder. *Fizikalna i Rehabilitacijska Medicina, 24*, 21-33.

[54] Badel, T., Kocijan Lovko, S., Podoreški, D., Savić Pavčin, I. & Kern, J. (2011). Anxiety, splint treatment and clinical characteristics of patients with osteoarthritis of temporomandibular joint and dental students - a

pilot study. *Medicinski Glasnik Ljekarničke komore Zeničko-dobojskog kantona*, *8,* 60-63.

[55] Badel, T., Marotti, M., Savić Pavičin, I., Zadravec, D. & Kern J. (2012). Radiographic validation of manual functional analysis of temporomandibular joint osteoarthritis. *Acta Clinica Croatica, 51,* 35-42.

Reviewed by prof. Vjekoslav Jerolimov, PhD, Zagreb, Croatia

INDEX

B

C

I

J

K

L

M

P

Q

R

S

T

U

V

W

Y